MASTERING LIFE

MASTERING LIFE

✦

Co-creating a Reality of Love
Through the Power of Sharing

By Ivonne Delaflor
Foreword by Alan Cohen
Author of The Dragon Doesn't Live
Here Anymore

iUniverse, Inc.
New York Lincoln Shanghai

MASTERING LIFE
Co-creating a Reality of Love
Through the Power of Sharing

iUniverse books may be ordered through booksellers or by contacting:

iUniverse
2021 Pine Lake Road, Suite 100
Lincoln, NE 68512
www.iuniverse.com
1-800-Authors (1-800-288-4677)

Cover Art:
Noe Delaflor
moches@masterylife.com
Cover Design:
Graphic Dreams & Magic
www.graphicdreams&magic.com

ISBN: 0-595-33291-9 (pbk)
ISBN: 0-595-66823-2 (cloth)

Printed in the United States of America

Dedicated to the volunteers of the
Mastery Life non-profit organization,
to all divine and self-empowered children of the orphanage La Casita de Cancun,
to all human beings living this miraculous
journey of Mastery, to Alhia and Christian
and especially to my husband
for his uniqueness, strength and Love.

The Sage does not accumulate for himself.
The more he uses for others,
the more he possesses of his own.
The Way of Heaven is to benefit others and not to injure.
~ Lao-Tzu

Contents

Part III   HUMBLENESS, REALIZATION, AND
TRUTH

Part IV   IT'S YOUR CREATION

Part V   *IT'S ALL ABOUT LOVE*

Part VI   *SERVE THY FRIENDS, SERVE THYSELF*

Part VII   YOU ARE A BUDDHA

Part VIII   MESSAGES YOU ALREADY KNOW

Part IX   CONCLUSION, ONLY FOR NOW

ACKNOWLEDGMENTS

I will like to begin by presenting my gratitude to M.C. Cannon and the teachings and guidance toward Mastery, responsible creation, and fulfillment of promises. Your guidance, spoken or silent, has been a major key in my life to choose love in all situations.

This book is the co-creation of simple wisdom of all the members of the *Mastery Life Newsletter*. We have compiled our experiences to share the journey of mastery we all are embracing in this lifetime. Therefore, I am thankful to you all. *This book is for you.*

I am grateful to all those beings focused on serving and loving others for the sake of love itself.

I am grateful to my children and my husband who constantly remind me of the purity of existence and the beauty of being on this planet. They always put me at choice with the challenges of relationships, the opportunities to grow, and the invitation to love through the daily basic experiences to bring mastery and balance within this blessed journey called Family.

I want to express my heartfelt gratitude to Alan Cohen. I feel humbled by the words he wrote for me in the Foreword and I must confess that often, when I forget who I am, I come back to them. I feed myself with divine inspiration and maintain my momentum with my intention to love and serve everyone.

Daily Guru, thank you for the continuation of your guidance, and for your selfless service for all you provide.

A thank you to all the Teachers who share their wisdom with us now and to all those who are going to do so in the future.

Thank you to all the children of the La Casita Orphanage for the divine opportunity to see the beauty of your eyes and divine courage. You are powerful teachers of Love for me.

To my friends who always remind me of the Mastering of Life with their examples, challenges, and faith in what I do and who I am.

Finally, thank you, dear reader. Thank you for bringing Mastery into your Life. I love you.

Ivonne Delaflor
September 2004

FOREWORD
by Alan Cohen

On the spiritual path, there are four levels of integrity. First, you talk the talk. Second, you talk the walk. Third, you walk the talk. Fourth and finally, you walk the walk. Ultimately, living an illuminated life comes down to just this: living, breathing, and shining the truth. Here, words are left behind or they show up to serve where they are needed.

I have had the honor to work with many extraordinary people on the spiritual path, including some renowned teachers and leaders. It is a special blessing to meet and co-create with people who model the lessons of love. Ivonne Delaflor is one of them.

I met Ivonne through serendipity—a series of coincidences that were clearly orchestrated from a higher perspective. She graciously invited me to present a seminar for her community in Cancun. Something inside me, an intuitive voice, guided me to accept her invitation. That voice has proven itself a miracle of God and good advice. From the moment I met this radiant soul I felt blessed and uplifted. Ivonne emanates a light so bright it can light an entire room. Her eyes and her smile speak of joy that arise from the soulful depth. She laughs often and embodies a rare combination of childlike joy and mature wisdom. In short, she is an Angel.

I am also deeply impressed by Ivonne's dedication to parenting and educating children. She displays a rare and highly focused intention to offer children the most optimal environment in which to learn and grow. I have watched Ivonne with her own children, those of others, and the children at the La Casita orphanage in Cancun. I am thrilled and inspired to feel the love and respect she shows them. Her kindness covers like a warm blanket and assures them they are safe and filled with infinite potential.

Now Ivonne has produced a wonderful book, *Mastering Life*—what a powerful title and theme! Don't we all want to be in charge of our journey and create according to our soul's desires? That is exactly what she maps out in these short, easy-to-read, and profoundly inspiring chapters. Her guidance is from the heart, filled with compassion, and dedicated to service—jewels for the spirit.

The lessons here, shared through essay, poetry, and letters keep pointing us back to the simplicity of loving. We find ourselves in a world where complexity seems to pull us from joy at every turn. Yet the return home, we discover, is not that difficult: fall in love with yourself, your beloved, your friends, your life, and God. Simply holding the consciousness of love will open doors that anxious striving cannot. Behold the answer that soothes, heals, uplifts,and changes the world, beginning with ourselves.

Take your time as you stroll through these insightful pages. Absorb the words and images and make them your own. While they seem to be teaching you, they are really reminding you of what you know deep inside your heart. Then bring the principles to life in your own unique way and enjoy the blessings they deliver.

Thank you, dear Ivonne, for all you share and most of all, for all you are.

The world is closer to heaven because you are here.

Alan Cohen
www.alancohen.com

INTRODUCTION

This book is the manifestation of three years of sharing between human beings from different traditions, places, and religions. The messages here are part of one hundred Mastery of Life free newsletters shared and created over the past three years. It is a collection of my writings and various letters in response to these writings as well as letters sent to me and my responses to those letters. I call this whole process co-creation.

Co-creation is what makes this book unique. I believe that the energy generated through interaction transcends words and messages alone. I am confident you will receive the transformational transmission of that energy no matter when it was originally written.

For it is through simplicity and wisdom, the power of sharing and a focused intention that one can quiet the mind, open the heart, and celebrate the majestic life bestowed upon all living creatures on earth. We have all worked very heart-close while keeping our mind and intention focused on mastering our lives. How blessed we all are to be on this journey, a journey of mastery and endless possibilities to create and recreate ourselves moment to moment, while alive on this sacred planet.

The experiences you are about to read changed many lives, including my own. This book does not take a scientific approach that utilizes studies and facts to tell a person how to be happy. Instead, this book uses the narration of personal experience to show a person what it means to be happy or to love.

The letters connect people together, which provide any person who reads them with something that is intangible but nevertheless very satisfying. Personal letters are intriguing; it is nothing fancy, and it's not full of scientifically proven methods to "improve" one's life. Instead, it is pure and practical wisdom, the honest sharing of many beings about their lifestyles, their emotions, doubts, and hopes for the miracle of being alive through the contemplation of quotes, ancient traditions, and daily human affairs.

Throughout this three-year process, I experienced a deep transformation in my beliefs, in my daily challenges, and a subtle and magical change in my hopes, dreams, and aspirations to serve the world in which I live. Different possibilities were presented to me through the sharing of so many beautiful people; sometimes the sharing was so intense for my own program that I needed to work on myself first to be able to respond to the sharing that served as an outlet for my voyeuristic nature. Through the process, I experienced a breakthrough and realized that we are all seeking the Guru who will enlighten us, the Master who will make our suffering disappear, and a magical formula that will change our lives, much like a fairy godmother in a fairytale. In truth, what we are looking for is already inside us. The wisdom of our fellow beings based on love, honesty, and integrity are treasures to behold of lessons, celebration, and mostly of love.

Please try to merge within the message by imagining you had written it. I know you are mastering your life most beautifully, most courageously and that you are doing the best you can as the miracle of love you have created yourself to be. Breathe. Remember you are here in this moment, alive on this planet called earth. Open up to assist us all in co-creating a reality of love through the power of sharing the love that you already are to make this planet a better place for our children, for future generations, and for the present moment in which you live, breathe, and love.

I welcome you now, and feel grateful for the opportunity to serve and share with you a journey of love through Mastering Life.

Ivonne Delaflor
September 2004

PART I
IN THE BEGINNING WAS THE WORD

*Beyond the words it is said
there is always a transmission.
I say unto you, beyond, above the words
and the no-words, all is the same divine light;
all is the same ever-evolving love.*
~ Ame

Truth

In every truth, the opposite is equally true.
~ Herman Hesse

The foolish reject what they see, not what they think;
The wise reject what they think, not what they see.
~ Huang Po

All experiences are as appropriate as my own; all choices are honored. We are all creating what we want in our lives: love, joy, fear, anger, worry, beauty. There are many possibilities and all are valuable for existence.

The more I stay with what I see without interpretations and judgments, the more I experience myself alive! These days I feel particularly free, for my choice is freedom within and my thoughts of freedom are creating my reality. I am experiencing the joy of being human and acknowledging my life as a human being on this planet. I choose freedom and love—love and more love. I choose to share my truth with you.

In truth, *truth* is who we are, what we search for, who we came here to be as love. Hiding and seeking truth are polarities. While we might play this game, truth is still the experience. Whatever we hide from others or ourselves does not relinquish the truth of who we are. For me, truth is not only a virtue; it is the experience of Source. Truth is what is happening.

In the midst of a moment, the truth manifests itself through the open gateway of trust. It is the simplest of events that trigger the creation of a thousand universes. When the mind is focused on the journey, one will never forget breathing the air, for the connection with the Divine resides in the wind's symbolism of life.

The gateway of the heart includes the miracle of healing. The connectedness with all occurs when the mind ceases to judge even that which is not. For the grandest of minds, trained with the most powerful focus ever—if there is no love—where is the reality they have created?

It is now in this moment that you all share the experience of Oneness. However, never, ever forget about the nectar of the gods, experienced only through the humbleness of accepting all that is and all that is not as yourself. Consciously sharing the Source that you all are is a gift for creation. There is no separation reverberating in the most subtle of your dimensions. Be aware of the gift bestowed to thy feet. Look in the mirror. Assistance, just as you have requested, has been granted. Breathe, be grateful and be whole, just as you are. Create the awareness of "Being Truth" and have the additional virtue of being you.

The Story of Your Life

When I hear somebody sigh, "Life is hard,"
I am always tempted to ask,
"Compared to what?"
~ Sydney J. Harris

A couple of days ago I was at a bookstore and overheard a couple's conversation. "I cannot believe it!" the woman said. "I am so depressed. I was not able, again, because of you, to go to the big sale at the store! Why, God? Why?"

The husband responded, "Well, if it wasn't for you, I would have had the black car I wanted instead of the white color that you liked!"

Then they began yelling at each other. "I don't know what I've done in my life to deserve this!" the husband shouted.

I did not stay to listen to any more. Yet, before I left the shop, I heard another man commenting to his wife, "Oh, those poor people. Life is so hard!" Immediately, something clicked in my mind and quickly, I made a list of what is important to me:

> Health
> My children
> The people I love staying healthy and free
> Being alive
> Love
> Smiles
> Love
> Freedom
> Love
> Forgiveness
> Love
> Gratitude

Love
Humbleness
Assisting others
Love
Growth
Celebration
Love
Laughter
Love
Truth

Is life hard? Of course, if you think it is! Is life joyous? Yes, the same applies! What we think is what we get. What we choose to believe as reality is what we manifest.

There was a time when I believed that I should behave in certain way in order to be liked. There was a time when I believed that I needed a guru or teacher. There was a time when all I cared about was going to parties and discotheques. There was a time all I thought about was traveling. I've noticed that along with my beliefs and thoughts, I have been manifesting exactly what I was thinking—positively or negatively. I've noticed that with my experiences, choices, and thoughts, I have been "writing with my thoughts, heart, and beliefs" the history, or shall I say; the story of my life.

One thing I found in common at all these stages of growth is that no matter how negative or positive the experience was, the most joyful moments—the ones that felt most real occurred when I was loving, serving, celebrating, and humbly grateful for whatever the experience was.

Create your own list of what is really important for you. Is life hard? You decide. I believe that life is an adventure, and love is the most powerful companion we have to accompany us in the creation and story of our lives.

SHARING:

Dear Ivonne,

I am writing today to share an experience that required a clear mind. I believe I am mastering life with this one. We shall see.

Three nights ago my oldest daughter got mad at me. I caught her smoking cigarettes and told her that she had broken an agreement she had made with me to stop smoking. She told me again that she would stop and the next morning I went into her room, found a pack of cigarettes and threw them in the garbage. Later that day, when she came home from school and found they were gone, she got very angry, demanded her cigarettes back and then hit me when I told her they had been thrown out. She was extremely angry.

I remained calm and did not react to the hitting and let her go up to her room to "chill out." About an hour later, she came down and told her grandmother in the next room that she had taken a bunch of pills and had cut herself on her arm. The next twelve hours were surreal for me. We called 911 because she told us she had taken thirty-five Tylenol pills. We went by ambulance to the emergency room where our family spent the evening waiting.

Luckily, the toxic levels were never extremely high because she either threw up quickly enough or miscalculated how many she took. They made her drink charcoal to remove all the toxins from her system and she spent a good deal of time vomiting. Once they determined she was okay medically, they called the child psychiatrist for consultation. It was determined that she needed to be admitted for evaluation and observation.

This was the hardest time in my life, to remain a witness when I thought I could possibly lose my daughter. I remained calm and felt detached through a good part of it. She was so angry with me for taking her cigarettes that she figured hurting herself would punish me. She did not realize the enormity of her actions; she never intended to kill herself. She just wanted to make herself sick so I would be sorry.

Through counseling, my daughter has realized how lucky she is to have the loving family she has and is very remorseful. The doctors have attributed most of what happened to her chemical imbalance combined with teenage hormones. She has taken a real tough look at what could have happened and what cigarettes do to your body. She says she never wants to smoke again and will never do anything like this again either.

I think it was all a positive experience. Her father, sister, brother, and I have all been loving and supportive through the whole process. Some of her roommates in the hospital have been raped and beaten and she got a real eye-opener as to what life is like for some people. That has helped her realize how lucky she is. She now says she wants more than ever to be a doctor so she can create an adolescent unit in our town and help others through their difficult times.

I am trying to continue to observe myself. Of course I did go through the whole range of emotions—guilt, fear, anger, sadness and joy—and I am sure I will continue to do that as my daughters and son grow. Right now, I am just extremely grateful that I still have teenagers that I can watch grow up and love.

All my love and honor to you,
Maria

Make a Wish

Health to enjoy the blessings
Sent from heaven;
A mind unclouded, strong;
A cheerful heart;
A wise content;
An honored age
And song.
~ Horace

A healthy mind, an open heart, a pure intention: these are gateways of love. These are the powerful tools to manifest with no doubt the possibilities of evolution and creation of more light and more joy for all. Heaven is everywhere, inside everyone. We are part of the existence of celebration. We must not lose ourselves in our own illusions or despair, but decide to walk wisely, transcending, evolving, and choosing love. At whatever age—an honored age—a song. Celebrate.

Being Fully Present

I am very aware that being fully present is a gift, but sometimes I cling to the past and to my expectations of the future. I do this in order to receive something in return when I give or do something for someone. This is a great reminder for me and may be for you, too. I compare the present moment to a child. A child gets totally mad or tearful one moment, but in the next, he completely forgets and embraces with fullness whatever is happening. He continues to play merged in bliss, not wasting time thinking about why he was crying or upset a moment ago. A child just continues to play, fully present in the moment. Let's use this as a reminder. Life is a present moment. It is neither short nor long. Life is simply life and eternity resides in the capacity of being present—of playing the game blissfully, joyfully and aware.

SHARING:

Dear Ivonne,

There are many times when I feel happy with myself but others may say or do things that make me feel bad or insecure as a person. How do I know what their intentions are and whether I should or should not avoid those people?

Mariana

---

1.   Used with permission of Osho International Foundation, www.osho.com

RESPONSE:

Mariana,

If the chicken sees himself as a peacock, it might also be that the peacock is watching himself in the mirror as a chicken. If it is true that the stillness is inside of you, then no action of others will move you from that place.

Every action and deed carries a wonderful opportunity for learning and manifesting more love. If you identify with the image of being a peacock, so be it. Be responsible for what that means. It is the same as identifying yourself with what others say or do. When something or someone hurts you or causes you to become upset, intentionally hold your breath and then begin to breathe again. Be aware that you are alive in the moment. Afterwards, try to understand if there is anything about that person that might resemble something you need to work on within yourself.

How will you know other people's intentions? By their demonstrated actions. How do you choose whether to stay or go? Always decide with the wisdom of your heart. Mastering your life with meditation will deliver clearer access to your heart. Be aware that if your intention is pure, then it is a blessing that others don't vibrate with the same purity of intention. Consider it a blessing that others generate dense things in order for you to let them go and create more space to allow someone else with a higher frequency and vibration to come into your life.

All things are as they are—being right or wrong is not really important. What is real and important is to acknowledge that all beings are gifts from existence. Through them, God loves you. Just remember, how you see yourself in the mirror of others' reflection is what matters. Just don't forget that it is only a mirror. Remember that what is real "is" you. The image speaks for itself.

By the way, while you are contemplating all of this, have a good laugh, and while you do, be attentive to who is laughing and why.

All my love to you all.
Respectfully,
Ivonne

The Parent Talk System Training

When quiet and still I hear the song of the butterfly.
She sings of freedom, spreading the colors of creation.
Choiceless her choice, she dances in delight
the song of its flight.
And when she flutters close to my heart,
I come out from my cocoon
and choose to be alive!
~ Ivonne Delaflor

I have just returned from an intensive workshop, "The Parent Talk System," led by its creator, Mr. Chick Moorman. This was truly an empowering experience of wisdom, practical tools, and enlightening messages for all parents, caregivers, and anyone interested in their own personal power and growth. I experienced many powerful, awakening, truthful moments during the weekend. Afterward, my heart was full of gratitude coming from both my capacity to choose my responses to the life I create and from my blessed bliss of being able to see and enjoy the surroundings of my creation.

Live and enjoy the journey. Love is love.

SHARING:

Ivonne,

When I hear the butterfly, I hear the song of transformation. We are all in the process of coming out of our cocoons. All places in that process have value. All are necessary. Where I am right now is valuable and desirable.

Thank you.
Mr. Chick Moorman
USA

RESPONSE:

Chick,

   Thank you for the reminder. I sense the light you bring with it, will bathe us all. It is an honor.

Thank you.
Ivonne

SHARING:

Dear Ivonne,

   Your poem melts my heart, for its words, for its transmission and because it comes from you. Every time I see a butterfly I think of Ame. Now, as I contemplate the poem, every time I see a butterfly, I will not only think of her, I will see in her the reflection of myself and my freedom to choose being free.
Thank you for the reminder. I love you very much.

Claudia
Mexico

RESPONSE:

Claudia,

   I love you, too, from the love and freedom that I choose to be.

Thank you for sharing.
Ivonne

SHARING:

Dear Ivonne,

   The other day I make a remark to a loved one that allowed emotions and angry feelings to make this comment painful. As soon as the words came out of my mouth, I was sorry, but it was already too late. Humbleness, which is not an innate quality of mine, helped me recognize my mistake and say, "I'm sorry" from the bottom of my soul.

Yes, we choose the words, but we need to use them to give and show love. It doesn't matter how hurt we feel sometimes. I think it was a fair lesson for me. I don't know if I make sense, but your letters makes me feel able to talk about it and I feel so much better now.

Gracias,
Patti
Mexico

RESPONSE:

Patti,

We all have experienced, in one way or another, what Patti is sharing with us. In addition, our response to the situation has created different emotions and thoughts. It is indeed a gift to have this type of experience. Without these experiences, how would we choose options that make us feel better? How would we know that we want to choose love, detachment, and kindness?

Existence is a beautiful game of many possibilities. We are all meant to be who we already are—evolution, love, and freedom. Remembering that everyone and everything is a gift, gives us the choice (if we choose) of what, who, and where we want to be. The illusion of not being there only reminds us of what we are and have always been. When the choice is love with an open heart, then humbleness, respect, kindness, and acceptance flows like our breath inside of us.

Patti, it was not the message that allowed you to speak up. It was you, only you, who, in an open state of heart, experienced the humbleness you truly are as a human being, as pure love, as yourself. Thank you for sharing. We all are on the journey—a journey of love.

Ivonne

Alone-ness

In the most intimate place of my soul,
I listen to the contentment of the journey,
delighting in celebration of the outcome of my creation.
When I breathe, I remember...when I am here, I am.
The emptiness of this contentment is full of this I am-ness,
and full of love, my choice to love.
~ Ivonne Delaflor

Since "The Parent Talk System" workshop, I've been having new experiences and insights into who I am, where I am, and who I want to be, as created by my intention, action, and thoughts. In this journey, I've encountered a very silent place inside of me. I choose to call it *alone-ness* not loneliness. This alone-ness is the generator of my intention to surround my life with people I love and the people who love me. Many of my illusions are in the process of shattering the reality I thought I was experiencing. I've made a choice, and the illusory catharsis and pain accompanied with it slowly vanishes when I remember my decision to love. I've made the choice of change, of evolution, always in the context of love.

Be full of awareness and full of choices from your power within.

SHARING:

Ivonne,

I can only hope that one day I find the peace that you seem to have within you. Today is not a good day for my husband and me. He is still in San Antonio at the university hospital undergoing more tests. I had to return home to face all the work waiting for me. Pray for him. He is having some minor surgery tomorrow. I only wish that I could be there with him, but I can't. I have no more sick days left, and if I take more, my paycheck will suffer.

My husband is a very strong and proud man. I don't think he would be as strong if he knew I was hurting, so I try not to show it and I hope, with God's help, he will be fine. He is too proud to have me there—he wants me to succeed at work. I miss him.

As I write to you, I have to hold my tears back. Trials and tribulations make us stronger. I am not worried about my strength. I just hope my husband can find his inner strength. Thanks for the poem and for your information.

God bless,
Olivia
USA

RESPONSE:

Olivia,

First, I am honored that you share yourself with me. I was going to write a big, enthusiastic motivating response to you, but suddenly I stilled my mind and realized what I wanted to say.

What is the struggle but the seed embracing its growth? For its destiny beholds the fragrance of the flower. While the turmoil of the wind and the power of the storm shake the soil where your seed is planted, the inner strength of its nature creates more leaves. The tall stem of the flower embraces life and with a smile its essence; the petals are shared with the rest of the universe. A peaceful moment waits inside the seed. It is its own nature. What the seed needs to grow, existence delivers. It is exactly what the seed needs to receive. Grow dear flower…for you are the seed of love.

Olivia, you are full of you. Share this love with yourself and others will courageously start to flower. Thank you.

Love,
Ivonne

Valentine's Day

> *Neither a lofty degree of intelligence,*
> *nor imagination, nor both,*
> *Go to the making of genius.*
> *Love, love, love, that is the soul of genius.*
> *~ Wolfgang Amadeus Mozart*

Yesterday I received a call from a person complaining about love. She told me she was too busy to tell people she loved them. She also said that nobody ever tells her they love her because she is too busy.

Don't set aside the grandest experience of being human because you are too busy! In the midst of your creation of your work, create the time to feel the love and express the love that you feel in the unique ways that only you know. Love is a miracle and so are you.

I truly celebrate the realization and the feeling of love created in my heart by recognizing that we exist. We want to evolve and grow into who we are and will always be. No matter what religion we choose, what race we are, whether we meditate or not, who we are is always love.

Today we celebrate Valentine's Day. People give presents or tokens of love to each other, so this day is a celebration of love. I was trying to explain this to my daughter but she decided it was better to continue playing. I stopped explaining when I thought she wasn't really listening to me and continued my chores.

Suddenly, my daughter began to sing: "Happy birthday to you. Happy birthday to you. Happy birthday dear Mommy and Daddy, and Christian and Alhia. Happy birthday to us!" I said, "Alhia, your song is very nice but today is not my birthday or Daddy's or your brother's or yours." She was unusually silent, which always gets my attention because it is so rare. Her eyes focused on me and then she said precisely and clearly, "Of course it is our birthday! Didn't you say that today we celebrate love?"

I leave my speechless response to your imagination.

Then she said to me, "Mommy? Why do we celebrate love only one day of the year?" She was right! Love needs to be celebrated every moment of our existence. Being able to love is a grand miracle and a grand gift.

Happy birthday to all of you as the love that we all are.

SHARING:

Dear Ivonne,

Children know, don't they, Ivonne? What a gift you gave her by not trying to talk her out of her knowing.

Peacefully yours,
Patti
Mexico

Looking for Love

I swallowed some of the Beloved's sweet wine,
And now I am ill.
My body aches, my fever is high.
They called in the doctor and he said,
Drink this tea!
Okay, time to drink this tea.
Take these pills!
Okay, time to take these pills.
The doctor said, Get rid of the sweet wine of His lips!
Okay, time to get rid of the doctor.
~ Jelaluddin Rumi

Why are so many people looking for love? They are looking for someone special or for something that makes them feel good. They are searching for someone or something outside themselves so that they can feel loved. Rumi's words support my personal experience of focusing on the love inside me and of acknowledging my own power within. Take whatever you need to understand. For a moment, your heart will join me in this whisper of love. The journey is created by you. Love yourself…follow your heart…that is a grand romance.

SHARING:

Hi Ivonne,

During the last fifteen years, I've been devoted to a female guru well known in New York. Following her teachings, I've been extremely disciplined in my activities, attending ashram functions and so on, focusing on every conscious aspect of a meditator, of celibacy, and the lifestyle of a nun. Last year, many people from all over the world came to the ashram, and at that time I met Will. Although he was very spiritual, he just wanted to meet my guru and then continue his spiritual journey. However, during his stay, our friendship transformed into major attraction and then love.

My fifteen years of devotion then turned out to be a grand limitation. When Will offered me his unconditional love and the opportunity to travel with him to meet other teachers and have many crazy adventures, I did not accept his invitation. I felt that in order to experience real spirituality, he should leave everything else, pursue studying with *my* teacher and stay with me. He chose to leave (now I understand why), acknowledging my choice and returned to his freedom and his life.

I thought I had made the right decision. Everybody was validating my choice so I felt pretty conscious about it. Some people, however, including my closest friend said, "Go ahead, and go with him. You never know when this experience will happen to you again."

Nevertheless, you know what? Things DO change! Three months ago, I received a call saying that Will had died in an accident. That call changed my life. My dreams were ripped apart. All my beliefs were pushed from my mind. Sorrow descended, followed by grand illumination.

Since that day, I love all who manifest in my life. I make wiser choices. I am more selective but more humble in my heart. I used to judge people who did not follow the same diet as I do or who did not follow or obey my teacher. I no longer consider the words "they are not conscious if…" I've chosen to break free of my own limitations. Now I say, "I love you" more often and experience a sense of fulfillment never felt before even during an intensive full-day workshop with my teacher. I make more mistakes, but I choose to learn faster from them.

I share this with you, for I felt such a powerful intention and purity of love in all the sharing of the Mastery Life messages. I knew in my heart that this was the perfect place to share my experience. I know it will assist some of you. I hope so. If by chance any of you are limited by a belief that is causing you to hold your tongue about speaking your love to the one you love, let it go! Scream I LOVE YOU!

I still feel a sad emptiness regarding Will, but his love was a big catalyst for me to choose freedom. Now I no longer choose to be the disciple I used to be. These days I'm a disciple of life, of my friends, of existence and myself. All and everything is my teacher. My focus is love. You never know where the Buddha is. You just never know.

I love you all as the same Source that we all are. Thank you so much, Ivonne and God bless.

Namaste,
Sandy
Ontario, Canada

RESPONSE:

Sandy,

Welcome to the Mastery Life messages. I am glad that you manifested here. Regarding your message, what can I say? Every journey is a gift, a land full of jewels and rich soil to love and to learn and sometimes un-learn. I do not have many words for your message. Just thank you, thank you.

Love,
Ivonne

Rest and Breathe

What a celebration the ocean experiences with the waves,
The perfect union of a leaf with the tree,
The beauty of a bird singing its tune,
Resting and breathing the essence of God.
~ Unknown

While on the spiritual path, aware or not, one must take rest to enjoy the abundance created with our intention. One must pursue with a pure focus of the mind, a positive way. One must delight in meditation while walking, writing, dancing, and eating. Rest does not mean stopping your work, but resting to breathe, to see and enjoy loved ones and this wonderful world. While on the spiritual path, we must be attentive to ourselves at all times, nurturing our spirit with kindness, compassion, and love. When a mother nurtures her child, she is nurturing herself.

Rest by being grateful and expressing it. Rest by continuing to do your best no matter what. Rest by walking your intention as your path. Rest your mind from daily noise. Rest your heart while loving. Rest your spirit while being present and enjoying the view. Continue walking and open your eyes to see yourself in the eyes of love.

SHARING:

Dear Ivonne,

What a wonderful experience we all had with the brilliant presence of Mr. Alan Cohen in Cancun. We focused our minds to the positive and beautiful energy that emanates from our souls. I have been with many teachers over the years, but they all ask you to look for the wrong. They speak about ego, about how closed your heart is and that you should open it. They speak of catharsis. They tell you what you should be doing, what you should be eating, what you should *be* rather that what you *are*, and so on.

However, Mr. Cohen did not do anything like that. Instead, he focused us all in the positive realm. The processes we worked through with each other were all positive and our hearts were filled with nothing but loving who we are and loving all others. Thank you for creating the opportunity to meet this wonderful being. I am not the same person I was.

Ericka,
Cancun, Mexico

RESPONSE:

Dear Ericka:

Thank you so much for your feedback. Thank you for co-creating the opportunity through trusting and assisting during Mr. Cohen's workshop. I am delighted with the recognition you have for yourself and feel humbled at your sharing. For me, Mr. Cohen's presence was a great mirror of humbleness, simplicity, and love. We had so much fun! Love is always in the air! We can have it all! We are all there is! We are the wisdom from our heart!

Ivonne

With or Without Words, Choose Love

I was going to type a verse from Rumi, a Persian poet, about existence, love and so on, when suddenly an ad appeared on my computer screen. It said, "Today I'm looking for a man. Join the club and get a free upgrade to the VIP room."

While contemplating this, I experienced a sensation of: What are we really looking for? Would anyone click on this type of ad? If so, why? Would they do it for entertainment or because it might deliver happiness?

Words are words. What we create them to be in our mind is what's important. God, Source, Consciousness, Enlightenment. What importance are you giving to words these days?

Maybe we could create a pop-up ad that says: "Today I'm looking for me. Join the club and get a free upgrade, while remembering that you are the VIP you've always been!"

Create yourself as you choose. Enjoy playing and have fun and remember to love. With or without words, choose love.

SHARING:

Ivonne,

Words are so important. Wouldn't it be great if everyone truly saw themselves as the incredible human souls they are? I try to help children see this all the time. Just the way our bodies work for us is amazing!

Have a great day!
Dixie

RESPONSE:

Dixie,

It is always great to hear from you. Yes, it is wonderful or full of wonder, the human beings that we all are. It is wonderful just as it is. Act as if everyone around you, including yourself, knows they are amazing, wonderful human beings.

I have the sensation that you could create a lot of fun with this. You will be astonished to recognize all the wonderful things you speak about in YOU.

With love,
Ivonne

PART II
IT'S ALL ABOUT CELEBRATION

The Master who forgets to laugh
or takes for granted the sunset;
he is ready for discipleship again.
For celebration, above all,
is the highest experience of enlightenment,
of Life…of Love.
~ Ame

Laughing with Joy

Imagine having a conversation with an embryo.
You might say, "The world outside is vast and intricate.
There are wheat fields, mountain passes and orchards in bloom.
At night there are millions of galaxies, and in sunlight
the beauty of friends dancing at a wedding."
You ask the embryo why he or she stays cooped up in the dark with eyes closed.
Listen to the answer, "There is no 'other world.'
I only know what I've experienced.
You must be hallucinating."
~ Barks and Moyne, The Essential Rumi

I like the way this quote reminds me how sometimes (or often) I choose to hallucinate. I get very serious about my beliefs, expectations, and desires and believe they are real! It also reminds me that "I am." I can choose to create myself as I wish and I am responsible for my choice and the outcome. It also inspires much laughter and that is really good. I mean, imagine the baby responding, "You must be hallucinating!"

Now imagine that you try to make others—your children, your partner, your family, your friends—see the reality that you are experiencing. Everyone is having his or her own experience. Each of them might or might not be creating a hallucination. Maybe they think you are hallucinating. We all are one and yet unique. So, laugh!

I am my experience, my creation, my intention, and many more possibilities. I see reality as I see reality. I experience my world as I experience my world, and it is okay. I suggest that whenever you create stress, struggle, or pain in your experience, imagine the dialogue and response of the baby in the womb, and with an open heart, say to yourself, "I must be hallucinating. I better choose love now!" Then laugh, have fun, and create a loving time. It is your choice. If you choose to hallucinate, whatever your hallucination is, I wish that it is a fun-full, love-full, joy-full one!

SHARING:

Dear Ivonne,

As the baby inside the womb implied, what we experience is what is real for us. At the same time, we are responsible for the creation of that reality. Maybe there are programs in our minds (from parents, family, school, mass media) that condition the way we experience that reality, which is, at the same time created by us. A good start then, is to be conscious about it and if those programs are no longer working for us, identify them, liberate them (get rid of them), and insert new programs that will set us free and guide us to be in contact with the beauty that we all are.

I love you very much,
Claudia
Mexico

The Power of the Mind

What you think produces energy in the universe,
if you think it often enough,
it will actually produce a physical result in your life.
Anyone experience that?
~ Neale Donald Walsch, Abundance and Right Livelihood

When I think of something—things, emotions, events—in a repetitious way, I have already manifested that in my life. When I was 17 years old, I knew many people, some of them friends that were having car accidents or surgery. I would continually think: I wonder what that feels like? What would I feel if something like that happened to me? How many people would come to visit me in hospital?

I would continue thinking like this, unconsciously aware of my power of manifestation, so that by the end of that year I had created it! I was involved in a major car accident that almost took my life. It left me with some important reminders about my power of manifesting and creating things!

I know this sounds radical but I like radical. Remember, we can create many things, emotions, events, with our power of thinking. If we choose to be aware of this power, my hunch (from experience) is always choose "positive thinking."[1] I consider myself a powerful manifestor of my reality. In my experience, what I choose to constantly think about has indeed manifested in my life. However, you know what? Love has been my grandest door for creating more love.

---

1. "Positive thinking" is the phrase made famous by Norman Vincent Peale in his 1952 best seller, *The Power of Positive Thinking.* "A positive mind anticipates happiness, joy, health and a successful outcome of every situation and action." www. successconsciousness.com/index

Believe in Your Power Within

Blessed by the mirror of the one I love,
Dancing with the music of my beloved's heart,
I choose trust and unconditionally I smile upon thee.
~ *Ivonne Delaflor,* The Soulmate Called God

Today I received a message from a friend reminding me of the joy of Love's game! Love, love and more love was my experience of this day, which began with a feeling of tiredness due to lack of sleep and a lack of decision to create an empowering, beautiful day. But somehow I remembered that I had a choice and slowly watched the sensation of heaviness and tiredness vanish. I made a choice to think positively no matter what the outside world or my physical sensation was like.

I continued with my positive thinking and like lightning, it struck me again—the awareness and the power of choices that come from within. The more we believe in it the more we create it as our daily experience. I immediately felt overwhelmed with joy and wrote these words:

Never, ever stop loving.
Have the courage to speak.
Be great-full.
Take risks.
Create a pure intention.
Manifest your intention.
Make things happen.
Love, love and love.
Create beauty-full reflections of yourself around you.
Be bliss-full.
Be with the ones you love.
Tell them how much you love them.
Trust.
Make healthy choices.

Assist others in remembering who they are.
Believe in your power within and choose to live in joy!

Now my friends. It is your turn. Believe in your power within. It is real. It is here. It is bliss. So be it.

Ordinary Miracles

Enlightenment is the biggest disappointment of all,
meaning that it turns out to be ordinary and accessible, not weird.
~ Chögyam Trungpa, Rinpoche

Where there is great love, there are always miracles.
~ Willa Cather

Creating miracles wherever we go.
~ Prema Baba Swamiji

I've always been attracted to the life and teachings of the Buddha, and I am currently taking a course called "Buddhism and Everyday Life." Today's lesson caught my attention. The words, "Enlightenment is the biggest disappointment of all" created a wide smile on my face. I caught myself thinking about enlightenment as being very sci-fi!

Enlightenment finds itself in our choices, in our wisdom, in our hearts. It is available to all. It is our true nature: a nature of light and love. It is available every moment.

You know what? The more I say I love, the more I create the experience of it. The more I let go of my expectations, the more I experience reality and the more my thoughts delight me in their absurdity for the purpose of entertainment. The more I realize you are reading the words I write, the more grateful I am that you all exist as the enlightened beings that you are.

True Beauty

Beauty is multidimensional.
To me, true beauty is opening to reveal yourself just as you are,
naked, without illusion.
Like everything else, beauty and ugliness are polarities that define each other
and are present within us all.
It is the embrace of the totality of us that to me represents a higher refinement of
beauty, the beautiful nature of Source itself.
~ Highest Creation

Today I received a special transmission of Source and Beauty that I will share with you. This beauty is eternal, like the fragrance of a rose, the perfection of the ocean, the delight in children smiling, a tear or a hug.

Many of us invest a great deal of our energy in that which creates more illusions or fantasies that take us away from the present moment and draw us into experiencing the realms of desire, judgment, comparison, and expectation! That is like trying to find beauty in what marketing directs us to buy to make us the perfect man or the perfect woman, forgetting in the process the beauty of nature, of a smile or a playful song.

It is time to think and let real beauty permeate your being. Look in the mirror. What do you see? Do you see True Beauty in its reflection? What is True Beauty for you? What is your experience? What does this tell you about who you are?

Contemplate that, write down whatever comes into your mind, and make a commitment during this week to carefully observe and be present to everything around you. Look, watch, and be attentive. Open the eyes of your heart and allow True Beauty to transmute your concepts of it.

We are Perfect

To love oneself
is the beginning of a life-long romance.
~ Oscar Wilde

Blessed are we who can laugh at ourselves,
for we shall never cease to be amused.
~ Anonymous

Life is good, love is delightful, choices are honored, and laughter heals. What are you creating these days? What are your concerns, your judgments and interpretations? See if they are as serious as you think. Make a choice. Look in the mirror. You are perfect just as you are.

A good laugh is good for the spirit, so laugh, laugh, and laugh some more.

This message is not meant for you to think a lot. Instead, it is an open invitation to wiggle, to dance and invite laughter not only into your mouth, but also into the sacredness of your heart.

Ha! Ha! Ha!

You are Me

The minute I heard my first love story
I started looking for you,
not knowing how blind that was.
Lovers don't finally meet somewhere.
They're in each other all along.
~ Jelaluddin Rumi

How rare and unique to find the gift of seeing yourself in your beloved's eyes! If you have experienced that, you know it is a precious experience. If you are still searching, remember that what you are looking for is already within you. Celebrate the possibilities of love. I've experienced this and although I have no words for it, "I love myself" would be my choice of words to explain this to you.

SHARING:

Dear Ivonne,

A friend of mine shared some of your messages with me. I'm sixty-four years old, and although I was born in the Ukraine, I have lived in the US for thirty years. I have always been a seeker of truth through different religions and philosophies and through my search, I found a spiritual teacher. She was from Denmark but attained illumination through the teachings of Sai Baba. Her disciples followed a Hindu path similar to East Indian teachers. We lived a simple, celibate lifestyle, focused on meditation. We wanted nothing to distract us from this structure.

I was her personal assistant for eighteen years, and three days ago I was called to her hospital room where she requested some private time with me. She said, "It has been revealed that an enlightened heart is the way back home. Forget about all I taught you. Find Albert and tell him you love him." (Albert was my dearest partner, yet I decided not to create a relationship with him since it would force a shift in my world "in my mind.") My teacher continued, "Live your life as a human being. Enjoy each sunset, and the craziness of the material world. Sell our Institute [in which we lived and where she held seminars for people from all over the world]. Tell everybody that I love them and that now they shall start living. When you have sold it and paid all our debts, the money that remains—keep it and travel. Find Albert and be a human being. You have enlightened your mind, now start living. You still have time. Don't follow anyone; follow yourself. Your heart knows the way."

Two hours after this conversation, she died. Her passing voyage gave me the best moment of my life. I woke up, from what? I don't know. I called Albert that same evening. He is a minister of a church and never married. I'm meeting him in two weeks time. I'm sixty-four and I've never felt better in my life. I wish that all young people on this path could dare to love as I am doing now. I don't know what is going to happen, but for the first time I feel free. Thank you for the reminders you send us all, Ivonne. I sense you have a grand destiny. Good luck.

Namaste.
Dhana
USA

Thinking of the World as an Illusion

Illusions deceive, colors circumscribe,
Even divisibles are indivisible.
~ Osho

Dear Friends,

I want to share with you the next story. Please write down your insights and see if any of this fits into your reality or the illusion you are currently creating. After writing, contemplate and then explore your insights again. This time make sure you write *only* what is real for you and what delivers love, joy, peace, and balance into your mind and heart.

Chuang Tzu is reported to have said that one night he dreamt he had become a butterfly. In the morning, he was very sad—and he was rarely sad. His disciples gathered together and asked, "Chuang Tzu, Master, why are you so sad?"

Chuang Tzu said, "Because of a dream."

The disciples laughed. They said, "Because of a dream you are sad? You, who have always taught us not to be sad even if the whole world causes you sadness, what are you talking about?"

The Master replied, "It is such a dream that it causes me very, very deep confusion, sadness, misery. I dreamt that I had become a butterfly."

The disciples asked, "What is so puzzling about that?"

Chuang Tzu told them, "Now, this is the puzzle: If Chuang Tzu can dream that he can become a butterfly, why not the reverse? The butterfly may dream that it has become Chuang Tzu.

"So now I am disturbed. What is right and what is wrong? What is real and what is unreal? Was it Chuang Tzu who was dreaming of becoming a butterfly or has the butterfly now gone to sleep and dreamt that he has become Chuang Tzu? If one is possible, then the other is possible."

It is said that Chuang Tzu never could get over this puzzle. This question remained for his whole life.[1]

---

1.   From *The Book of the Secrets*, used with permission of Osho International Foundation, www.osho.com

The Glow of Love

I ne'er was struck before that hour
With love so sudden and so sweet,
Her face it bloomed like a sweet flower
And stole my heart away complete.
~ John Clare

The glow of love, how wonderful and shiny it is! I saw an old friend this morning. It had been five years since we last saw each other. I was shopping in a store where you can get all sorts of meditation[1] tools: CDs, incense, Buddha statues, and so on. He was buying a silver OM symbol necklace. I recognized him and we were happy to see each other. We chatted for a while and updated each other about our lives, and when we were saying farewell, he said, "You know what? I want you to have this OM necklace. I just feel the need to give it to you." I was speechless, for only a few days before, I had sent a gift to a very special being and it was the same OM necklace that he gave to me. This was a beautiful moment of synchronicity and a beautiful message of love.

What you give is what you get. This is especially true if you believe it. The glow of love is everywhere—in a memory, in a gift, in the synchronicity of events.

Look in the mirror and visualize your heart glowing in any color that you choose. Imagine your heart speaking to you. What does it say? Let's all create more love in our own way. Let's share the glow of this love.

---

1. "There are various types of meditation—prayer is probably the best known, but there is also Transcendental Meditation, mindfulness meditation, Zen, Buddhist and Taoist forms of meditation." www.holistic-online.com

Understand

Existence is illusion.
Understand, go beyond sorrow.
This is the way of brightness.
~ The Dhammapada

I saw a T-shirt in a store that said, "The only thing real is you." What do you think? How do you know what is real or not? By judgment? Comparing data? How? Is it enough that it is real for you, or do you seek validation in order to create your reality as you experience it? This moment is real for me.

SHARING:

Dear Ivonne,
    I would like to understand more.

Austin
USA

RESPONSE:

Hey Austin,
    I know you would like to understand everything. I would like that too. You know what? I've come to the realization that there is nothing to understand and that all—except you—is illusion.
    Am I confusing you more? Good! That is the point of existence: to confuse you so much until you give up and then you really begin to understand everything. You have a very intelligent mind, but here is the trick for you: You are very spiritual, and in this spirituality resides your uniqueness and truth. You are different from other people and so am I. Sometimes in your life, the illusion that being different is wrong will appear in your mind. However, you know what? It is a gift to not be a part of the herd.
    It happened to me a lot and sometimes it still happens. I used to care and cried a lot. After my accident, I somehow became stronger than ever. I did not care

that my arm looked different, although other people did. Well, to be truthful, sometimes I did care. Now, when people are mean or resentful or make jokes about me, I have fun with it. It is better to be hanging out alone than with a bunch of unconscious, robot-like people who are not interested in real life!

I like you a lot. You are a very powerful being. I would like to invite you to do an exercise, but it is your choice. Every morning when you wake up and at night when you go to sleep, look at your reflection in a mirror. Look at your eyes and try not to blink at all. (If you do, it's okay.) Practice this for seven days and then tell me about your experience and I'll give you a new meditation. The only guideline is that you must do it twice a day, consistently over a period of seven days.

This is all for now. We'll see each other soon.

Love,
Ivonne

A New Landscape

The real voyage of discovery consists, not in seeking new landscapes,
but in having new eyes.
~ Marcel Proust

Make the most of yourself,
For that is all there is of you.
~ Emerson

Making the most of who we already are. Does this point to the possibility of experiencing more of ourselves? What is your experience of "making the most"? For me, I choose to change the word "make" into "create." Create the most of your heart, yourself, your life, everything.

While meditating, a very special friend and I had a beautiful experience of communion, synchronicity, and detachment. I opened my eyes and saw the current events in my life in a different way and found new light, possibility, and mastery through them. Things I thought were locked into a certain form were transformed in shape, flavor, and color.

May you create this day in whichever way you choose. Open your eyes and through your heart see more of who you already are. The landscape is beauty-full; it has been created by you.

PART III

HUMBLENESS, REALIZATION, AND TRUTH

*A humble one is he who recognizes the Divine work done through him as a bowing
from the Divine itself
toward all human beings.*
~ Ame

Serious Spirituality

Unless and until man stops seeking escape
from his ultimate destination by losing himself
in the childish play of illusory pleasures,
he cannot grasp spirituality seriously.
It is time to stop playing with the scintillating toys of illusion
and yearn for the attainment of the One and Only Reality.
~ Meher Baba

Who or what do you think is the one and only reality? What is Meher Baba referring to as the "ultimate destination"? What is serious spirituality?

The time has come to deliver the gracious state to your heart. Move on or stay. The wise one knows to move *with* the waters and not against them. Surrender and love like a child with the awareness of being *One*. Demonstrated actions speak for themselves. Set yourself free from control, from desires and limitations. You are living now, you are alive. Look at your face, have a good laugh. You are never alone. Never forget to enjoy the continuous blessings from existence.

I am serious about that.

SHARING:

My dearest Ivonne:

I reach out to you with the awareness of our Oneness and the deep respect, love, and admiration I hold for you in order to share the following thought-feeling: You can't always be funny, you can't always be smart, you can't always be witty, but you can always be loving and you can always be respectful.

Dearest angel, I'm approaching the steepest part of my journey. I am strong, I am blissful and I'm ready for more.

Mauricio
Mexico

RESPONSE:

Mauricio,

You can always be who you are.

You can always be free.

You can always smile through your heart and your bliss.

Keep on loving!

You can always be more of this.

Thank you for the love and the transmission of who you are through your words.
Ivonne

SHARING:

Ivonne,

Here are my answers to your questions:

1. *Who or what do you think is the one and only reality?*

The only reality is "what is." Human beings cannot experience one reality because their perceptions pass through filters of desires, expectations, experiences, their own history and individuality. A human being is destined to "watch" this one reality, "what is" through its limited subjectivity.

2. *What do you think Meher Baba refers to as "ultimate destination"?*

The ultimate destination is enlightenment and acceptance of limitations.

3. *For you, what is grasping spirituality seriously?*

Enjoying intensively this unique experience of existing as an individual. Using our senses, experiencing, giving oneself to life and to love, love and love.

Paco
Mexico City

RESPONSE:

Paco,

Thank you for your message. Love, love and love. For me, this is the one and only reality. It is the delight of the journey and the power of Source as the power of *One*.

SHARING:

Ivonne,

Many of your sweet messages have left me savoring, with delight, the delicious words you choose to send. This last message has shaken me and provoked the true feeling of reflection. It comes at a time when I feel myself at a crossroads. I have decided to take charge of my life, start loving myself a little more each day, and follow my true intention.

"What are you waiting for? Wake up!" This is what Meher Baba's message says to me. Illusions have been a big part of my life, to the point of confusing me as to what is real and what is not, believing that all the non-real was real and continuing to live without really living. I can no longer pretend to be asleep or pretend to not know where my true path is. I have placed myself on my true path of reality. I have awakened with a hangover, (dreaming is certainly intoxicating) and I am on my way. With guides like you and the power of choice, I am choosing a reality that brings me closer to discovering the truth of who I am each day. I love you and thank you for being part of my journey.

Elsa
Acapulco, Mexico

RESPONSE:

Dear Elsa,

Your message is a reminder for me to Wake Up! I celebrate your choice—definitely a choice of love. Yes, I am part of your journey because we are one. Thank you so much for sharing your truth. It is very empowering for me to read and feel your response. It serves me as a meditation and as a way to focus my intention of light. I am really grateful.

Namaste.
I love you as myself.
Ivonne

Be Humble and Truthful

Be humble,
For you are made of earth.
Be noble,
For you are made of stars.
~ Serbian Proverb

Truth, call my name.
I stand naked before you,
Stripped of illusion.
~ The Mayan Oracle

What is the experience of humbleness for you? My attention is called to the experience of truth as a whole, balanced experience. We are required to be truthful, to express our truth in the words we say, but mostly to become the truth of who we are and who we came here to be.

Being truthful requires that you accept all that you are—dark side, light side, fears, limitations, all and everything as part of the experience of who you choose to be. The experience of truth must start with oneself. How can you demand truth from another if you are not truthful with yourself?

My meditation teacher recently said to me, "Never compromise your truth." As he said it, an earthquake occurred in my being. It was a new awareness and more power within manifested in the contemplation of this transmission. It came with the relinquishment of any illusions that I might be creating as distractions.

Be truthful with yourself.
What do you think it means: "Truth, call my name"?
What do you understand as: "I stand naked before you, stripped of illusion"?
What do you want to create as truth in your life?
How do you want to create it?
What would you like to heal?
Who would you like to share this with?
Do you really want to be truthful?

What is the experience of truth for you?
Are you aware that you are already Truth?

Be courageous and from your power within manifest a more truthful you through the power of your heart!

"Reality"

There is no way you can use the word "reality" without
quotation marks around it.
~ Joseph Campbell

SHARING:

Dearest Ivonne,

How much joy I create when reading the messages you send. Thank you. I am a Reiki therapist and chiropractor, and many patients benefit from my healing work. When I received your last message, I was about to treat someone who had had a lot of back pain for many years. I decided to repeat in my mind, as a mantra, the contemplation that you sent. I kept on repeating it until something happened that my mind does not want to understand: For a moment I could not see my patient anymore—he had disappeared! I thought I was going blind. I thought it was a delusion. Then something in me stopped and there was a warm sensation of clarity, oneness, and fulfillment. I became love, the humbleness in which I am made of. I began breathing very fast and became aware that I was holding my hands over my heart!

I had completely forgotten about my patient for five minutes. When I came back, I was about to explain and apologize to him. Just before I started to speak, the man said, "Is this a new technique of yours? I just had the most amazing experience of my life. You disappeared, and the pain in my back disappeared for the first time in years. I saw myself as the sky and the stars. Thank you, Doc."

Dear Ivonne, there is no need for a response from you. You've already responded with your intention and sharing and I must admit that I am afraid of your response. Thank you for the focus you represent as a challenge for me. May you continue in your journey just as you are doing.

Tom
USA

RESPONSE:

Tom,

Thank you for sharing your experience. It is timely and appropriate as all experiences are. I just want to share a story that my first meditation teacher told me.

"A child was sitting under the tree of abundance. When he was hungry, the tree delivered an apple exactly into his mouth. When he was cold, the tree shared leaves to cover him. Whatever he wished for was delivered to him directly into his hands: food, love, warmth, health. Whatever was needed just came directly to him from the tree of abundance. The child kept on receiving more and more and more until one day he turned to the tree and asked, 'Why me?' And then the tree disappeared!"

Stay with this story and enjoy what the tree is giving to you.

In love,
Ivonne

Waiting

The same soul that enlivened Mother Teresa, enlivens you.
Do you truly want to spend your golden years
in ever-increasing fear and isolation?
Don't you secretly dream of giving your life away in pure unselfish love?
There are people waiting, next door and around the globe,
waiting for the power of your love.
~ William Martin, The Sage's Tao Te Ching

A friend told me yesterday about a conversation she overheard: "I don't have time right now for relationships; it requires too much focus and it distracts my mind. I'd rather be working and doing what I am supposed to do." What a gift she gave me, for her words helped me to contemplate my heart.

In my experience, there is no greater joy than assisting others, being in love, and loving "another." There is no grander sense of fulfillment then when one feels helpful and of service to someone in need. It is true what some people say: "It all comes back to you tenfold!" Give and share your love; many beings are waiting. What are you waiting for?

Celebrate

I never lose sight of the fact that just being *is fun.*
~ *Katharine Hepburn*

It is a happy talent to know how to play.
~ *Ralph Waldo Emerson*

I wanted to create more fun and celebration in my life and the lives of my children and friends. So yesterday in my Meditation-In-Motion class for children and their parents, I used the affirmation, "I am Celebration." If you had seen the joy and brightness in these children's eyes, I assure you, you would have melted in the moment. Imagine seeing and feeling and watching them playing and dancing! The adults played and danced, too—even more than some of the children. It was a great moment for everyone.

The idea is to have fun, be fun. Celebrate life, have a laugh! Jump! Dance! In this moment, wherever you are, realize that you are alive and that you are a player of Source, playing your own creation, celebrating love.

SHARING:

Dearest Ivonne:

I woke up and I found a message on my soul's answering machine. It said: "Hi! This is God. We are going to share responsibilities and divide our tasks today. I am going to take care of your problems while you focus on loving yourself and the people around you. Call me tonight to check on how we did! I love you."

Mauricio
Mexico City, Mexico

RESPONSE:

Dear Mauricio,

Did he call you, too? Wow! God as Source is really keeping up with all of us, isn't he? Did you call him back? Create more fun in your life!

I love you as myself.
Ivonne

Create a New Game

You can discover more about a person
in an hour of play than in a year of conversation.
~ Plato

If life doesn't offer a game worth playing,
then invent a new one.
~ Anthony J. D'Angelo

You know, whatever is happening in your life and whoever is included in your creation, my suggestion is to keep on choosing love. Many people want to focus their mind and have the concept of enlightenment feature strongly in their belief systems. However, what I would like to transmit to you is my experience regarding the power of choosing to be a positive loving experience yourself. Practice it today. Manifest kindness in your life. Be humble.

Know that where you are is just where you create yourself to be. If you do not like it, then change it! Transform it into a new face of love and see yourself in your creation. Keep on loving! Isn't love the grandest gift you can deliver to yourself?

Focus your mind, but never, ever forget the power of an open heart! Keep on having fun. I hope you are creating here and now, a fun, celebratory existence, discovering constantly who you are while playing this game of Source called Life.

SHARING:

Dear Ivonne,

I am contemplating what *play* really is. Isn't everything play if you look at it the right way? When I am working at my computer I am just playing with letters. The words: "work," "play," "having fun," or "being bored" are just words that you choose to color your existence. Therefore, you are right. Choose to have fun, choose to play and enjoy every moment. Then it all becomes a big game.

I started running about three months ago. I run three miles, three times a week. I am always pushing myself to run faster, harder, to get my time down and so on. Sometimes it is hard and I am not having fun. I always feel great when I am finished but about halfway through it's tough.

Recently, Danielle (my youngest angel) started exercising with me and I had an interesting experience. She cheers me on, tells me I am doing great, encourages me to keep going and go faster. She makes me laugh, and just having her there has transformed the whole experience into having fun instead of just pushing myself to get through it. Now, I look forward to the days I run because I know it can be playful and fun. Children are always having fun and playing, and if you ever find yourself being too serious, you should drop everything and go be in the presence of a child. It will transform you and your world.

All my love,
Maria
Virginia, USA

RESPONSE:

Maria,

Thank you for your sharing. I can tell that your child within is creating lots of fun with the reflection of your own children as yourself. Yes, everything is play—a Source-full game and choosing to see it that way makes a lot of difference. Keep on playing wherever you are. Keep on looking forward to running and running toward forever. Keep on playing through love, a more power-full you.

Gracias,
Ivonne

God Within

The seed of God is in us.
Pear seeds grow into pear trees,
hazel seeds into hazel trees,
and God seeds into God.
~ Meister Eckhart

I hope you are still continuing with the Celebration of your life as Love in a fun way.

Consider these questions:

1. Where do you think your true power is located?
2. Do you believe in "God" existing outside of yourself?
3. What is your true nature?

SHARING:

Ivonne,
Galaxy Lady,

You caught me awake! To answer your questions:

1. *Where do you think your true power is located?*

My Power is being alive. Life through sanity gives me the opportunity of having power for anything else.

2. *Do you believe in "God" being or existing outside yourself?*

God is Love and resides in me and in anyone that acknowledges it this way. Through residing in me, God resides in life, because I AM LIFE and this IS, and it is inside me and inside all that I perceive. The same IS, is inside anyone and anything they perceive.

God is the ocean and its waves, the refreshed sand by the whiteness of the wave, the wind and the breeze together subtly or with intensity, the birds that slide in it, the colors of the sunset. This is God. There is God.

My seven-year-old son loves to look at the colors of this natural painting that God paints for us so close to the sea each day. One day he asked, "Daddy, do you see that sunset?"

"Yes," I said.

"I would like us to be inside that sunset, covered by its colors."

I was astonished. My emotions slipped out of my throat. They went to my eyes, my reason and my soul. I could barely respond, but I said, "We are there my son, because here and now we are alive, living, with God. We are being-feeling the sunset."

"Oh, yes, yes, we are!" My son cried with joy.

We held hands and continued being-feeling in silence with God and life—both of us, the three of us, the four of us together inside the sunset. All of us—my son, God, Life and I—we were one.

3. *What is your true nature?*

Living life with physical, mental and emotional sanity. Loving, loving me, to love.

Receive a kiss,
Juan
Acapulco, Mexico

RESPONSE:

Dear Juan,

I created a big smile on my face when you chose to share with us your wisdom and experiences. I agree that God as Source is all there is, as I am as well. Source is God. The Source that we recognize as God is eternal and always creating itself. We are the same Source, the same beauty, the same power.

Your son is very connected to the oneness and divine essence of creation—as all children are. He invited you to merge and disappear forever through existing always as One! Thank you for sharing the reflection of who you are and the power of Source that resides in your heart.

I celebrate your God within,
Ivonne

SHARING:

Ivonne,

I loved it! Life is a Banquet! It is a Party! It is a Celebration like everyone experienced in your meditation class! We must not allow everyday life to kill that extraordinary feeling! Let's celebrate and enjoy life!

Love,
Patti
Acapulco, Mexico

RESPONSE:

Thank you, Patti, for your sharing. Yes, life is a celebration, a banquet, a party! It is so powerful that nobody can kill it. Next time Mr. Everyday Life shows up, invite him to the party. Ask him to join the Celebration, the festivity of who you are and whom you create yourself to be every moment of your existence. I assure you that Mr. Everyday Life will have no option but to melt and become this Celebratory game himself!

All my love,
Ivonne

SHARING:

Dear Ivonne,

Thank you for today's beautiful message. It's so true and we need to keep remembering this.

In celebration of all of us,
Kia
USA

Partners in Relationship

True Partnership is achieved only by separate and whole beings
who retain their separateness even as they unite.
The Path of Partnership can lead you to the realization
of a still greater union—union with the higher Self, union with the Divine.
~ Ralph H. Blum, The Book of Runes

In my experience of unconditional love, I've found that the more I accept myself and let go of my expectations and desires, the more I manifest Love as an experience in my life. I feel a growing acceptance for all and everything and acknowledge that all the beings in my life are unique and free to be just as they choose to be.

Mr. Blum's wisdom speaks to me of the true nature of relationships—of the possibility of Love available through wholeness and freedom. The more whole we are, the more balanced we will be and the richer our relationships manifest. We then create our partnership as Portals of Love—possibilities and new experiences for our own evolution.

When you come to the realization that everyone must journey through whatever experiences they choose to manifest, you cease to cling to the desire of control, the emotion of missing, and the sensation of loneliness. You manifest the grandest acceptance and celebration of knowing that all the ones you love simply exist as yourself in the here and now, embodied as human beings. For my experience, even if I am not physically close to them, this is enough! Remain true to yourself and love, love and love!

SHARING:

Ivonne,

Validation and more validation. Just yesterday, I was reading a book written by Jerry Jampolski about relationships and how a holy relationship is based on unconditional love, respect, trust, and freedom. How many times do we hear that in a partnership, women and men complement each other, and then instead of looking inside ourselves for the wholeness that we all are, we believe someone outside of us has that something we lack. Therefore, we go on searching for something we already have. Each of us contains the yin/yang. Each of us has the potential of being whole, holy. Once we understand this, we will be able to recreate holy relationships and through our uniqueness and these holy relationships, we can merge in a greater communion with God.

I love you.
Claudia
Mexico City, Mexico

RESPONSE:

Dear Claudia,

Thank you for your sharing. I believe that yes, we all have the potential to be whole. It is our nature, it is our destiny, and it is in our power to create this as a constant in our experience with our choices.

Whole fully,
Ivonne

Treasured Moments

*Life is not measured by the number of breaths we take
but by the moments that take our breath away.
~ Unknown*

What moments in your life have "taken your breath away"? For me, some of the moments that connect me to the Source of Unconditional Love and at the same time remind me that I am breathing are:

> my son's laughter
> my daughter's joy
> my teacher's wisdom
> a sunset
> a rainbow
> a smile from the one I love
> waking up in the morning and breathing the new day's air
> hugging a tree
> saying I love you
> praying to God

I invite you to write down at least five people, things, actions, or events that remind you of the joy and blessing of being alive. Carry this paper with you wherever you are. See this as an emergency tool. Whenever you feel sorrow or despair, check out what you wrote and remember. Also remember that what you wrote is not only to be read in times of pain. It is also helpful to remember not to take those things for granted in times of success, happiness and joy.

Now, breathe, delight and love. Look at yourself in the mirror and touch your heart with your hands. There is no one better to take your breath away than the image reflected there that is telling you that you are a human being and that you are alive.

PART IV
IT'S YOUR CREATION

There is a sparkle of magic in the realization
that this moment,
the same present one
in which you are living in the here and now,
is totally created by you.
But it takes a peaceful mind
to surrender into this awareness.
~ Ame

Dare to Love

The man of Love is the man of trust,
and the man of trust is the man of truth.
~ Osho

Love should not be postponed for a single moment.
Postponing Love is postponing life;
Postponing Love is missing the opportunity.
~ Osho

I have just returned from a seminar introducing the "Parent Talk System" to teachers and parents at my daughter's school. During this first day of the seminar I found many parents were concerned about their children behaving appropriately—acting in a certain way, eating certain foods and so on. They are all very focused parents, interested in learning to teach children about "life." Nevertheless, I found that very few were choosing the experience of love as the main guidance for whatever they wanted to transmit to their children. Many parents thought that showing love or demonstrating love was a sign of weakness. I find this experience manifested not only in parents, but also in many human beings, young and old. Yet, experience tells me that life through love is a beautiful manifestation.

I believe that love is, above all, a gift to oneself and a powerful gateway for the creation of beauty, expansion and joy. Love, from my experience, has been the grandest fuel ever to create myself as I am now.

Celebrate love, be love, dare to love. Do not postpone love. If it is happening here and now, it is for you to delight in and merge with as the love that you are.

Love yourself,

Love your life,

As you are Love.

SHARING:

Dearest beloved angel:

You have pointed out that the most prevalent obstacle to happiness that exists in our civilization—dare I say our planet—is the postponement of love. The fulfillment of life's promise is only achieved through love: self-love, love of others, love of nature and love of the divine wholeness that permeates everything that is and binds us as one.

We are taught to restrain love, to save it for a special person and certain family members, and maybe a few select friends that have passed the most stringent selection process. Furthermore, we are encouraged to show and profess love only on certain days and at appropriate moments. What a shame!

Love is the nature of our human-ness. It is the force that propels us onto grander and more pure stages of being. Love and its daughters, Respect and Compassion, are the saviors of our race, of our wilting planet.

It is time to stop postponing love. Stop shelving feelings and start sharing this Divine Magic with everyone. It all begins with a smile on our face and a "Have a blessed day!" to strangers we encounter on the street. The rest is not that difficult.

Love purely, unconditionally, without expecting reciprocity. Love wholly, sincerely and without fear of the consequences. Love with all your being, not only your heart. That is, use your wonderful mind to direct and deliver the vibration of this love most effectively. Love yourself. Love yourself. Love yourself. I will not postpone love. I love me. I love you.

Mauricio
Los Angeles, California, USA

RESPONSE:

Dear Mauricio,

Source, Love and more of this love is what I read beyond the message of your words. Keep on loving yourself. Keep on embracing love, here and now as the sun embraces the earth, as the rainbow embraces the sky.

All my love,
Ivonne

SHARING:

Ivonne,

Interesting how parents see love as a weakness. Yet, saying no, can be done with love. Holding a child accountable for their actions can be done with love. Setting limits can be done with love. Parents sometimes equate love with giving in, saying yes, and letting kids have their way, but it is so much more than that.

Lovingly,
Chick Moorman
USA, author of *Talk Sense to Yourself* and *The Parent Talk*

RESPONSE:

Chick,

Thank you for sharing your wisdom with us. It is indeed appropriate. What you say applies not only for small children but also for bigger children (usually called grownups).

I once read in the *Dhammapada* that kindness is the way to defeat meanness. This is reflected in your words. Setting healthy limits through respect, kindness, and love opens more possibilities for creating an affirmative life, not only in others but also for ourselves.

May you continue as a Healer, through the empowerment and source of your words.

In Love and Service,
Ivonne

Enlightenment through Relationships

Your love contains the power of a thousand suns.
It unfolds as naturally and effortlessly as does a flower,
and graces the world with its blooming.
~ *William Martin,* The Couple's Tao Te Ching

Have you ever contemplated the possibility of enlightenment through relationships? I've heard so many people on the spiritual journey say this is not possible. Many well-known sages went to caves to meditate and isolate themselves for years in order to become "enlightened."

I wonder if the experience happening here and now on this planet is about being in relationship with other human fellows. Isn't there a grand possibility through their reflection to choose more of ourselves and enlighten our minds and generate more love?

Enlightenment through relationships can happen but you must be ever vigilant, keeping your intentions as pure as possible. You must detach from any judgment, interpretation, or expectation that you might have of another, whether they be your lover, son, daughter, wife, husband, or friend. Remind yourself constantly that all and everything is a reflection of who you are—as Source, as bliss, as the endless possibilities that you can create yourself to be.

Focus on your relationships as a gateway of Love and Source. See the love that you are through their eyes and create more light in your experience. See what manifests. You might even be surprised how many Buddhas or enlightened beings you find on your way!

Choices

The Truth of your choices will create ripples of endless love for you and many.
What it seems will evolve into a higher purpose, a higher love
experienced only by those willing to transcend the illusion of time,
creating wholeness and delight wherever they go
always through the Gateway of the Heart.
~ Ame

I believe that if I choose love as the experience of the moment, more love comes back to me. If I choose positive thinking, I experience and create more positive things in my life. If I move beyond my mind and focus on my heart, I see an enormous gateway for me to experience more love, more joy and more bliss. What I am saying has nothing to do with others—it has to do with or is related to the experience in the here and now of who I want to be, what I want to create myself as, and which experiences I choose to have.

So go ahead, remember it is all about choices. Create ripples of love that expand in your heart, transcend illusions, and keep on loving—no matter who or what, always starting within yourself.

Mind Your Own Business

We know nothing of tomorrow.
Our business is to be good and happy today.
~ Sydney Smith

Lately I've been watching my world and I see how some of my reflections create a struggle of *doing* rather than *being*. Whatever I see in another, I see in myself and from that, I make a choice. These last few days I have been indulging in the game of "forgetting" and focusing my energy and attention on *why* questions. Why did he or she do that? Why did they choose this instead of that?

It happened that when I made the choice to focus my energy on creating a detachment from these questions, a friend sent me this quote by Sydney Smith. Bingo! A big stone hit the core of my being and created ripples of certainty and constancy in my emotional choices and immediately I made myself a promise:

> *I will mind my own business. I will be truthful and kind, choosing happiness here and now in the present moment. I will let others mind their own business, create their own choices, and honor whatever they want to create themselves to be.*

Now, if you choose to do so, take my advice: Mind your own business, take care of yourself and be happy here and now. It is your total responsibility. Nothing is lacking. There is nothing you need. You have the capacity to love, to be happy, to be you.

SHARING:

Ivonne,

Smith's quote is of primary importance for my existence and for those that have stopped using drugs or alcohol. "Today exists only today, for today." Yesterday the wind is already gone. Tomorrow is only a breeze that hasn't yet come.

Being happy here and now and always is not a business; it is not our business. It is simply a beautiful equation, an opportunity bestowed to us by life. It is a gift delivered in consciousness by God, for "tomorrow" will be "today."

Receive a kiss,
Juan
Mexico

RESPONSE:

Dear Juan,

Thank you for the beautiful reminder. Indeed being happy is not "a business." It is our nature; it is our soul. It is, as always, Source.

All my love,
Ivonne

God Alone is

A poor devotee points to the sky and says,
"God is up there."
An average devotee says,
"God dwells in the heart as the Inner Master."
The best devotee says,
"God alone is, and everything I perceive is a form of God."
~ Ramakrishna

All experiences are appropriate. God is everywhere and in everyone, as Source, as Love. Yes, God alone is. Everything perceived is a form of God. One can only see what one is. We are Source. All I see is a reflection of myself. All I am is Source. I Am.

SHARING:

My dearest inspiration,

I just talked to my dad and he said, "You should go to church and pray to God." I told him I talk to God every day and he responded, "Yes, but in the temple you can find all the positive energy related to God." I replied that the temple is the whole universe. He didn't understand. He went on, "You should listen to God's message contained in the Gospels." I told him I listen to all the signs and symbols that God sends me in one way or another in my daily life, and that was that.

I just wanted to share this with you.

With profound love,
Claudia
Mexico

RESPONSE:

Claudia,

All experiences are appropriate. Now, just as your father did, I'm going to tell you to yes, go to church, but you know what? Go to the church in your heart, where you will find not only the positive energy related to God, but you will also find God Himself beating through you! The whole universe is inside your soul. Listen to the holy messages; listen to the whisper of Source through your own love.

Wherever you go you are taking God with you. Invite your father to this church. Let us see what unfolds. God alone is.

All my love,
Ivonne

Thirsty for More?

Desires achieved increase thirst like salt water.
~ Milarepa, Drinking the Mountain Stream

Have any of you ever been distracted from living here and now in the moment, for the pursuit of desires or expectations? A couple of days ago a friend called and said, "Even though I am aware that cheating on my wife creates dense energy between us, my mind and my desire to date more women and have sex with all of them, grows every day. The more I create that, the more I am thirsty for that, but the sorrow grows deeper along with the fear of losing my wife."

Do you think we deserve to live in fear, to live feeding the cycles that create the illusion of separation? Do you think that we should continue living with the thoughts of a past that is not here anymore? Should we fulfill ourselves by always focusing in a not-yet-lived future?

Let us increase our thirst for love and kindness through the focus and practice of good deeds, positive thinking and meditation.[1] Let others live. Respect their choices while continuing to choose love. May the water we drink be of kindness and respect. May we all be satisfied with who we are in this moment. Whatever we desire outside of ourselves delivers temporal mental satisfaction, but the inner thirst to love more, serve more and just be in this moment, brings contentment, fulfillment and no thirst at all—only more love.

---

1. "In addition to the growing body of research literature on meditation, physicians, psychotherapists and other professionals are increasingly adding meditative techniques to their practice." www.holistic-online.com

What Lies within Us

What lies behind us and what lies before us
are tiny matters compared to what lies within us.
~ Ralph Waldo Emerson

What lies within us contains the whole universe, all the grandest powers, and all that is as what we are. I just finished reading *The Initiation* by Donald Schnell, and something within me was deeply moved and intoxicated with bliss. The reflection of an enlightened being's journey moved within me the most sacred and celebratory validation of who I am. It was not the book itself or just the words. It was what was within the words that validated in me the most pure intention of my heart to love, love and love through the focus and sharing of another's experience as my own. Go within as much as possible and from that place look in a mirror and let me know what you see.

SHARING:

Hello Ivonne,

A friend of mine shared your messages with me. I melt each time I read them! I love your responses, your work, and the things you recommend. I was wondering if you could guide me in choosing a spiritual teacher. I plan to go to live in the US for two years and I have heard there are many good spiritual schools there.

Merci, and thank you, thank you, thank you.
Danielle
Lyon, France

RESPONSE:

Dear Danielle:

Thank you for your words. I feel your motivation. I believe, though, that you are the only one who will find the right teacher—probably when you least expect it. He-she is waiting for you right now. Just be attentive to the teachers in your life that you have now, before your teacher appears. Remember that this moment is the only moment you have. Enjoy it, celebrate it, and learn from all the wonderful experiences as your only teacher, as the only one. "When the student is ready, the Master appears." Just keep your focus, meditate, be blissful, be loving, be you. Whatever school resounds strongly in your heart—pay attention. Follow your heart, your nature, as Source, as God and remember that your teacher is already inside your being.

Respect-fully,
Ivonne

SHARING:

Ivonne, my dearest angel of love:

Everything is a reflection of who we are, of what lies within us. The words, the message, the intention contained in these messages are a mirror of the beauty that you are. What has moved in you are your own cells vibrating at the recognition of your own divinity.

Dearest angel, when I read your messages and see through your pure heart, I also see through your reflection the beauty of who I am. Thank you for being my mirror.

I love you very much.
Little Grand Soul, Claudia
Mexico

RESPONSE:

Dear Claudia:

As always, your constancy and the beautiful truth that you share with us delights my heart. I am grateful for the reminder you are for me. I reaffirm to you that whatever you see, feel, or think of another is indeed who you are as well. We are mirrors of endless possibilities for each other, reflecting Source, no matter the form, time or space.

Much respect and as always, much love,
Ivonne

What Would Life Be?

We cannot all see alike, but we can all do good.
~ P. T. Barnum

What would life be if we had no courage to attempt anything?
~ Vincent Van Gogh

All are reminders, all are reflections of who we are and what we want to create ourselves to be. Whatever the intention—call it courage, trust, truth—it leads us to the same path, the path of being whole, of being who we are.

What would life be if we were not aware that who we are is God itself?

What would life be if there were no colors?

What would life be if there were no questions like this?

Think about it. While you do, be sure of one thing: Existence will not be the same without you.

What would *life* be without you?

The World Arising in Me

When the world arises in me,
It is just an illusion:
Water shimmering in the sun,
A vein of silver in mother-of-pearl,
A serpent in a strand of rope.

From me the world streams out
And in me it dissolves,
As a bracelet melts into gold,
A pot crumbles into clay,
A wave subsides into water.
~ Ashtavakra Gita *2: 9-10*

I particularly love these ancient words, poetic and inspiring. It offers a lot for my heart to contemplate. The words speak of merging, of oneness, of subtle energy, of love. It is said that the universe resides inside each one of us and the experience we create of it and from it depends on our choices and the way we see our creation—call it life, call it experiences, call it the present moment. We all are, in essence, the same oneness—we are the wave and the ocean—we are not separate as human beings from the earth or the universe—we are it all. We all merge from the same Source, from the same clay. We are the shimmering and the light itself. We are the world.

Without Desires

There is pleasure when a sore is scratched,
But to be without sores is more pleasurable still.
Just so, there are pleasures in worldly desires,
But to be without desires is more pleasurable still.
~ *Nagarjuna,* Precious Garland

It definitely feels good to scratch a mosquito bite, but it feels eons better to be still, attentive, loving, and aware, accepting moment to moment what is, who we are, as we choose to be.

SHARING:

Ivonne,

I have created so much misery in my past because of desires. As you have said, they brought only temporary satisfaction. When I woke up from the illusion, what was real was gone. Today I live my life with the welcoming and acceptance of what happens in the moment.

I once had a wonderful Guru, Osho, whom I was lucky to meet while he was alive. He always embraced his disciples with so much love and truth. He used to rip away any desires of his disciples by just smiling at them. When Osho died, I felt lost. I am 52 years old now and I have come to the realization that if one wants to experience "being alive," one must drop desires and transform them into acceptance. My teacher and my heart taught me this. This is my story.

Great newsletter, Ivonne. I feel great energy through it.

Namaste,
George
New Zealand

RESPONSE:

Dear George,

Great teachers, kind words, here and now, transforming desires into acceptance and love. Great learning, great guidance.

Thank you,
Ivonne

Silence

Just as a mother would protect with her life, her own son, her only son,
so one should cultivate an unbounded mind towards all beings,
and loving-kindness towards the entire world.
One should cultivate an unbounded mind, above and below and across,
without obstruction, without enmity, without rivalry.
Standing or going, seated or lying down, as long as one is free from drowsiness,
one should practice this mindfulness.
This, they say, is the holy state here.
~ Sutta Nipata

I implored the sage in earnest last night
to unveil the mysteries of the universe.
He whispered softly in my ear,
"Silence! It is something to perceive but never to say."
~ *Jelaluddin Rumi*, The Life and Thought of Rumi

SHARING:

Dear Ivonne,

This is such a lovely quote from Rumi, so poetical. I found out about it some time ago when I realized there was too much noise in my mind coming out most of the times through my voice, until I had enough of the misery. I have come to the understanding that it is only through silence that one can reach the light in oneself. It is only through silence that one can listen and perceive the beauty of divinity.

Thank you.

Love,
Katia
Playa Del Carmen, Mexico

RESPONSE:

Katia,

An image of light came into my mind with your words and a warm sensation to my heart. Continue with your relentless focus. Thank you for the reminder.

Love,
Ivonne

PART V
IT'S ALL ABOUT LOVE

Once again…a simple message,
the one that carries the history of all avatars
and enlightened beings of all times:
It is Love and only Love—the true nature of God.
~ Ame

God is Everywhere

As the air is everywhere,
Flowing around a pot
And filling it.
So God is everywhere,
Filling all things
And flowing through them forever.
~ Ashtavakra Gita *1: 18-20*

Imagine Brahman as a sea without shores.
Through the cooling love of the bhakta,
some of the water becomes frozen into blocks of ice.
Now and then, God assumes a form and reveals Himself to his lovers as a Person.
But when the sun of Knowledge rises, the blocks of ice melt away
and God is without form, no more a Person.
He is beyond description.
Who could describe Him?
Anyone who tries, disappears, unable to find his "I" anymore.
~ *Ramakrishna,* The Wisdom of the Hindu Gurus

What beautiful reminders these ancient words are for our hearts! Their wisdom is as refreshing as breath itself. For truly, we are full of God—expressions of Source, existence and creation. All is this sacred presence. Whatever we see as opposite is just an illusion. All and everything is God. All religions, all beings, everything, everyone, are God and love. If we could all stop our beliefs in separation for one single second, we would have a taste of oneness, of connectedness, of the reality that we are the all and everything of creation.

Beyond description, I acknowledge the love that you are and celebrate you all, one more day on this living planet called Earth.

Feeling Lucky?

Depend on the rabbit's foot if you will,
but remember it didn't work for the rabbit.
~ R.E. Shay

I used to be a true "believer" of power outside myself, of Mrs. Luck creating something for me or not. Mr. Chick Moorman, author of *Talk Sense to Yourself,* assisted me in creating an inner earthquake to alter my concepts regarding myself. I created a new realization: I found that Mrs. Luck was inside me. Believing in something outside myself tasted or felt good, but only temporarily, (I call it my power within.) This realization had to do with who I am, what I choose to create, how I feel more positive and loving, and at the same time, more powerful (in a compassionate loving way). It is what I choose to believe myself to be.

If you think the rabbit's foot will work for you, then really focus your mind in creating that miracle. If it happens—whatever you wished for—ask yourself, what was the power that made this dead rabbit's foot work for me? Who manifested it?

I suggest you make use of the most powerful Mrs. Luck amulet this week—the power of Love, or you can call it God, if you prefer. The sharing I selected to add here is a message I received from someone who doesn't agree with anything that has been shared before. I want to acknowledge our unity in diversity and celebrate the appropriateness of each thought, each experience as unique and valuable for existence.

SHARING:

Dear Mastery Life,

A friend of mine sent some of your messages to me and it is with grand sadness that I see people are just losing their way. They are not following Jesus Christ and the scriptures. What causes me the most rage is how people think they are powerful or that God lives within them. It is absolute nonsense! Everyone is a sinner. You all need to carry a cross like me. Suffering is the only salvation. You cannot create mastery in your life; you can only be a servant of the Lord.

Goodbye.
Julio
Puerto Rico

RESPONSE:

Wow! Julio, thank you for expressing your beliefs with such select words. I am particularly fond of radical truth, (or what I interpret it to be). I acknowledge your sacred presence and with grand joy, I receive your words. Beyond that, I celebrate that you exist, for you truly show there is choice as to what to believe.

Here are some of the insights I want to share with you:

1. If you believe you are carrying a cross or you are a sinner that is probably what is being created in your reality. I suggest you rest for a while in carrying the cross of negative thoughts. Your load might get a little lighter.

2. If you believe suffering is the only salvation, please clarify and explain what we need to be saved from.

3. I haven't yet met any sinner on my way through planet Earth. I've just met people making different choices. So any of your "sinner friends" that you have encountered, please let them know that they also have a choice not to be a sinner.

4. With your own words, "You can only be a servant of the Lord," I give you something to contemplate: "A Master is a servant disguised." Thank you for your sharing.

In the service of Love and light,
Ivonne

Take the Plunge

What can be gained by thinking about the scriptures?
What fools? They think themselves to death with information about the Path,
But never take the plunge!
~ Ramakrishna

You shall go out with joy and be led forth in peace.
The mountains and the hills before you shall break forth into singing,
and all the trees of the field shall clap their hands.
~ Isaiah 55:12

The time has come, dear souls from light and of light, to vibrate with one heart, one intention and one same focus: *Love.* The healing of planet Earth is essential. The need for courageous souls daring to love all is vital. Children need this beautiful planet to re-create itself again through the unique power of Love. They need an earth that shines brightly in Love, a planet where trust can be experienced for safety of the purest of beings.

Many people believe this is only work for saints. However, God lives inside all of us and everything you see. This is expressed as love as well through the power of creation and manifestation. All are God. You are all there is. Be responsible for the part you play in your world. Create choices that vibrate with the highest possibilities for your evolution.

The time has come and if you are reading this message and feeling at least a little opening in your heart, you will recognize this is meant for you. Let's create life as a conscious celebration of its creator. Let's celebrate this planet as the home of all of us as One. Celebrate yourself. Choose the highest expression for your own happiness. Healing starts with a smile. Healing happens when believing happens. Healing is when you are aware that all you need is Love.

No Enemies

Am I not destroying my enemies when I make friends of them?
~ Abraham Lincoln

Love is the higher grace that permeates all and everything into the Oneness that we all are. Feeding darkness with darkness makes it grow. Speak, think, and be attentive only to density and that is what you will attract and create. Speak, think, feel, and see love and that is what you will create as your experience.

Let's give light to darkness, love to hatred. Make friends inside yourself—that is where you start first. Give love to yourself and allow yourself to be loved. The mind is not an enemy, neither is the ego. Just feed yourself with love and the rest will follow.

What is "forgiveness" to you?

Create a friend-full time with yourself.

No Matter What, Always Choose Love

The more I choose to love, the more light permeates my heart.
The more I share my heart, the more I love you as one.
No matter the appearance, I will always love you.
We are One.
~ Ivonne Delaflor

Yesterday a special friend closed all communication with me because I made the choice to meet with a new spiritual teacher rather than the one we both shared for some time. While honoring his choices, there was sadness in my mind, although love kept permeating my being.

You have probably had experiences when you thought certain situations were unfair or persons in your life were making inappropriate choices. Remember, all choices are appropriate and valuable for existence. All is Source. From my experience, a choice to keep loving, no matter who or what, is definitely a most profitable investment of the heart.

Today I invite you to pray, meditate, or contemplate—whatever you call it. Pray today for love for everyone—for yourself, for the planet, for animals, and for all children so that *all* can feel love and be the love that they are for a moment. Create a beautiful image in your mind and use your imagination just like a child. Imagine for a moment that all the darkness—all the density—has been transformed into the purest love ever—into the love of God.

A friend of mine said to me, "I do not turn love on and off like a light switch. I am not made like that. It is always on." The choice of my sweetest friend was to keep on loving, no matter what. Do not turn off your love switch. Find a way for yourself to make sure the love switch is always turned on.

I wish for you a glorious, love-full day, letting go, setting yourself free.

The Taste of Sweetness

A king asked a sage to explain the Truth.
In response, the sage asked the king how he would convey
the taste of a mango to someone who had never eaten anything sweet.
No matter how hard the king tried,
he could not adequately describe the flavor of the fruit,
and, in frustration, he demanded of the sage,
"Tell me then, how would you *describe it?"*
The sage picked up a mango and handed it to the king saying,
"This is very sweet. Try eating it!"
~ Hindu Teaching Story

How can I describe what love is or what God is? It is a personal experience. I could give you many explanations and yet the words would only be limitations. I can only say to you that for me, love is when my children are healthy, when my beautiful teacher-husband is happy, when I see a baby's smile and the gorgeous sunset. Love is writing this message to you. I could also say that God is all of these things.

Just as the sage gave a mango to the king for him to taste, I come to you with an open heart in my hands. I love you. We are One. Taste love by loving others. Be kind, honor others' choices. Taste the mango, taste existence, taste God.

Love is your birthright.

Behold God

In the valley, on the mountain, I beheld only God.
In hardship, I saw Him by my side.
In ease and well being, I beheld only God.
Like a candle, I melted in His flame.
Amid the sparks of the flames,
I beheld only God.
~ Baba Kuhi of Shiraz, Rabi'a the Mystic

God is as life, as Source, as friends, as all that is and is not. God is inside, outside, and everywhere, as a belief or disbelief. God is the beating of your heart, the hope for a better world, healing energy. God is the powerful force that cannot be described with words. God is truth. God is peace. God is love. God is a word that can encompass all and everything: female, male, spirit, human, nature, *all and everything*.

Trust and be held in this power and create a wonder-full life.

Good Apples and Bad Apples

God is Love and God is All Good, and it is we, not God,
who create the unlovingness and suffering.
We do this when we distance ourselves from God,
when we separate ourselves from our divine nature.
It is not a movie to watch, as some truly misguided people say.
It is a stage upon which we choose to play a part.
To give love is to express God, through our words, actions,
and creative efforts, or to laugh at the pain of others,
turn our backs to their grief and ignore that people are suffering.
~ Swami Leelananda

Gurus who preach celibacy while secretly engaging in sexuality,
present sex as an esoteric initiation ritual or advanced spiritual exercise
that must be kept hidden.
It is the lie, not the sex, that's the real issue.
The lie indicates the guru's entire persona is a lie,
that his image as selfless and beyond ego is a core deception.
~ Joel Kramer and Diana Alstad, The Guru Papers: Masks of Authoritarian Power

I recommend never adopting the attitude toward one's spiritual teacher
of seeing his or her every action as divine or noble.
This may seem a little bit bold, but if one has a teacher who is not qualified,
who is engaging in unsuitable or wrong behavior,
then it is appropriate for the student to criticize that behavior.
~ His Holiness the Dalai Lama

There is a lot of confusion and judgment regarding gurus and their "expected" behavior. Prema Baba Swamiji points out the phrase "good and bad apples" in his wonderful book, *The Initiation*. Neither is better or worse, but he simply states the fact that some apples are not suitable to eat. This applies to our daily choices regarding mentors, books, teachers, workshops, and so on. Choosing the most positive apple—the healthiest one—must be preferable to choosing a rotten apple. Whatever choice is made, there is always the opportunity to heal from the experience and choose a better apple next time.

Create a loving time and eat lots of good apples. Hang around with flowers, not thorns, no matter how conscious or enlightened someone might appear in your mind. Just be happy. Just Be Loving. Simply Be.

SHARING:

Dear Ivonne,

I am the vice-president of a worldwide Spiritual Congregation led by an internationally recognized teacher. Lately, I've been trying not to see things that happen at our ashram. I have been seriously contemplating my role here. More and more I see people frightened of my teacher, and I see they are all robots. It might be my projection, but I don't see many happy people around here anymore. I've witnessed many unfair acts disguised as "everything is appropriate" or "the play of consciousness" or "the polarities and density of…," and so on. However, I don't see much love around here. Please do not give my name.

Thank you.

RESPONSE:

Thank you for your message. Lately, I've been hearing lots of stories like that. Remember, "A teacher from the heart is a teacher like no other." A child is a good example of that. Choose Love. Meditate as Love. Enjoy the world, breathe the air, smile, help, serve. Choose respectful words. No harm. Just Love.

Namaste,
Ivonne

SHARING:

Ivonne,

What are these weeds doing in my garden? Today, as I drove my lawn tractor over weeds more prevalent than the grass I had been trying to grow, I asked myself, "God, why are all these weeds growing? What's the significance of them in my garden?"

Deep inside my heart, I heard God talking to me. He said, "My dear, what is a weed? It's only your perception of the plant that makes it a weed. What makes this plant separate from the roses you treasure so much? They are both green and produce oxygen to sustain your life. That is why in my garden there are no weeds. It's all in how you choose to love the plant."

I began to reflect on the words I heard so clearly in my heart. Suddenly, I realized that in life we choose to look at some people the same way we look at the weeds in our garden. It is our choice how we wish to perceive them. What makes them good or bad? Who are we to judge who is good and who is bad? We are all one within God's eyes. All people are similar, just as the weed is similar to the rose. When we choose to love unconditionally, the weeds soon become flowers in God's garden.

Stay with God,
S.S

Service from Friends

The only service a friend can really render
is to keep up your courage by holding up to you a mirror
in which you can see a noble image of yourself.
~ George Bernard Shaw

Truly, what are friends for? They mirror us—what we like and dislike of our own being. They reflect the love that we are, and deliver the possibility of *choice*

I had a very interesting experience last week while visiting the Pyramids of Chichén Itzá.[1] After witnessing an ancient Ritual of Love guided by a recognized archeologist, my mind had the most wonderful experience. My perception shifted and my imagination became innocent. Each of my friends there had his or her own personal experience of the sacred ceremony. After the visit, we shared our experiences, and as I contemplated what had happened, my mind went quiet when I recognized the reflection my friends had towards me. They all coura-geously held a mirror of Truth in their hearts! All their experiences were mine. All that they long for, I have in my soul as well.

The most important part for me about this gift of visiting the pyramids in a private ceremony was to be able to share it with friends. Beyond any concept or any interpretation of the mind, I saw and felt deep love for them. Above all, I came to the realization that where we are, as we are—in this same moment—is the most divine ritual, the most sacred sighting. The most powerful teacher lives in the here and now, through our hearts, as friends, as reflections of each other. It is in this moment that love and creation are happening through the power of sharing and the love from God. I honor you, dear friends, for reflecting back to me the Divine Essence of your Heart.

---

1. Chichén Itzá is the ancient city whose name means "in the mouth at the Itzáe's Well." In its time of grandeur (between 800 and 1200 A.D.) it was the center of political, religious and military power in Yucatán, if not all of southeastern Meso America. www.internet-at-work.com/hos_mcgrane/chichen/chichen_index.html

The Face of the Universe

When we look into our own hearts
and begin to discover what is confused and what is brilliant,
what is bitter and what is sweet,
it isn't just ourselves that we're discovering.
We're discovering the universe.
~ Pema Cordón

Discovering the universe is discovering God—through the love of the children of the world, through the love of nature, of planet Earth, and the love of all.

If you were face to face with Jesus, Krishna, Buddha, or Muhammad right now, what would you say? What one question would you like to ask them?

SHARING:

Dear Ivonne,

To come face to face with Jesus, it is not necessary to come face to face. It can happen at any moment in our hearts and in our minds. The meeting and the conversation with Jesus is just as real as if he were standing in front of us. The questions I would ask today are: "Were there times you didn't want to be a hero? Were there times you felt like you had no choice but to go on being someone who others look up to and follow? Was that a responsibility you chose or one that the times and circumstances dictated? How did you deal with that?"

Chick Moorman
USA

SHARING:

Ivonne,

First, we have to assume that our awareness was sufficiently developed to recognize a Buddha or an awakened one. Even in Jesus' time, most people did not recognize that he was a world avatar.

I suppose many people would ask questions or requests of the Buddha. My request would be, "Please bless me with your love, healing energy, and spiritual wisdom so that I may serve as an instrument, like you, to relieve the suffering of those in need. What one hand can do, many hands can do more easily. Let me be an instrument of this grace." This is also my prayer for the moment and for this here and now. In the words of St. Francis of Assisi, "Allow me to be your instrument."

Dr. Donald Schnell
USA, author of *The Initiation* and founder of the Power of Love Foundation

Certainty

Give up what appears to be doubtful for what is certain.
Truth brings peace of mind, and deception, doubt.
~The Prophet Muhammad, as reported by Hasan bin 'Ali

The heart knows! Look at children—they move with their hearts, they play with their feelings; their trust is unconditional. The truth that a child *is*, is unmistakable. It is pure certainty. Many people are afraid of truth. Many speak about truth—even teach about truth, yet often their actions are quite different from what they say. Other people will be very truthful when speaking, but when it comes to listening to their own truth as spoken by others, they might hide or get upset.

I believe that truth includes kindness, right action, patience, respect, a willingness to learn, to make mistakes and mostly an open heart to love. If you want to live more in love and more truthfully, you know exactly what to do and what not to do.

Look at your eyes in the mirror. What do you see? Who is looking back at you? What are those eyes telling you? Behold the power of truth. Look at yourself. What type of life do you deserve? What are you creating? What are your priorities? Money? Fame? Success? Love? What are your priorities in the here and now? Do you feel certain of them?

Go within. Contemplate these questions with an open heart and eyes of truth. I love you for the truth that you reflect back to me.

PART VI

SERVE THY FRIENDS, SERVE THYSELF

*Nature serves all humans
in the most unconditional way…shouldn't all
have learned by now the same divine practice
to experience the same
with another brother?*
~ Ame

Spreading Love

Go out into the world today and love the people you meet.
Let your presence light new light in the hearts of people.
~ Mother Teresa

After the verb "to love," "to help" is the most beautiful verb in the world.
~ Bertha von Suttner

I agree, I believe, I feel, and I choose to live and become Love and share it with everyone I meet. I share love, even mentally, even with someone I don't know—thinking love, speaking love, walking love, sharing love, being love.

Love!

Please, what harm will love do to you? Spread the word of love through your actions, through your kindness, and through your heart! Light a heart! Bring light to your heart!

I don't know about you, but for me, assisting others in whatever way possible is a gift. Helping without wanting anything in return except the contentment and happiness of the one you serve is an incredible offering. Giving without expectations, loving without demands, letting go by giving, loving, being—those are what I try to do. I believe that helping and assisting others is just a disguise for "self-help." Truly, what you give is what you get! The Beatles sang it beautifully, "All you need is love" and "A little help from my friends."

I love you all. Yes, I do.

One's Own Nature

Truth is enough. Remember that. Truth is all you need.
Just as there is one sky, which covers everything on Earth,
so is there one vast truth, which covers all your needs.
This is inspiration, but is also practical fact.
Truth is enough.
~ The Daily Guru

Although there are countless teachings that instruct
how to obtain enlightenment in a future life,
almost all of them are nothing more than expedients.
As the ultimate instruction, there is simply no teaching that is superior
to the true practice of the awakening to one's own nature.
~ *Hakuin,* Zen Master Hakuin

A teacher's talk included, "Never forget that falseness can be very attractive and
charming, like a pit covered with colorful flowers." In their misunderstanding,
people mistake attractiveness for rightness, only to wake up too late.
Wake up now and prevent a fall. See how practical this is?
~ The Daily Guru

Truth is enough. Love is truth. Love is enough and so are the words, I love you. Thank you for reading this. Let us keep on praying and letting God, as Truth and Love, work through us.

Meditation
Devotion
Service
God
Truth
Awareness

Consciousness
Love
Right Actions
Right Deeds
Right Words
Respect

All of these concepts are the same. It is who we are, it is our own nature, it is the practice of that which we are—that is what makes enlightenment possible.

Enlightenment? Awakening to oneself? Sounds like a joke, but it is the only awakening. It is right inside our hearts. Many teachings will assist and guide you on a path you will find very familiar—a place where you will say, "Hmmm, I think I've been here before." It is a place called The Divine Destination that you so much long to arrive at. Here you will find one person, one moment, One, only one—yourself, your heart, and your own Power to Love.

If you were awake or enlightened at this moment, would your experience be different from what it already is? Think about it!

SHARING:

Dear Ivonne,

In the 1960s, Ram Dass[1] taught, "Before you are enlightened, you chop wood and carry water. After you are enlightened, you chop wood and carry water." What Ram Dass was trying to convey was that enlightenment was no big deal.

From my own experience, enlightenment is everything. Before enlightenment, I was more or less on automatic pilot. If those around me were gossiping or indulging in negative thoughts and actions, I joined them. Before enlightenment, if others wanted to drink alcohol and abuse their bodies, I joined them. I stuffed my body with meat, dairy, eggs, white bread and sugar. I was overweight, out of shape and unhappy. I was a man who didn't know how to hug, how to love or how to cry. I was indifferent to God's love for me. Today, I love God with all my heart.

Do I still chop wood and carry water? Yes, I do. Am I different? Yes, I'm healthier, happier and more content. I don't believe that enlightenment is some-

---

1.   Ram Dass (Servant of God). A worldwide recognized spiritual teacher who traveled to India where he met his spiritual teacher, Neem Karoli Baba in 1967 who inspired him to change his life and the lives of many others through good deeds and love. http://www.ramdass.com

thing that is attained as much as a process of continual self-improvement until nothing but Self remains.

Thank you.
Dr. Donald Schnell, author of *The Initiation*, and founder of the Power of Love Foundation

Train Yourself

This itself is the whole of the journey.
Opening your heart to that which is lovely.
Because of their feeling for the lovely beings who are not afraid of birth and death,
aging and decaying, they are freed from their fear.
This is the way you must train yourself.
I will become your friend and an intimate of the lovely.
To do this I must closely observe and embrace all states of mind that are good.
~ Samyutta Nikaya

Positive thinking[1] is the power to choose to see the lovely, the divine, rather than the opposite. Why do we give power to negative expressions of life? Why do we often give power to past memories or grief? Why do we choose those things when we always have the choice to see the positive and lovely things happening here and now? Observe and embrace all states of mind that are good and also those which are not so good. Watch your thoughts in order to choose. Ask yourself: Do I really want to have this not-so-good thought? What are my options?

Be attentive as a constant witness to yourself as much as you can. Remember that you are already doing your best. Give your power to that which makes you love, share, and be loved. Watch the negative aspects of your mind, but do not give them your power.

You have a choice—to be love, to see love, to feel live and to live through the power of Love.

---

1. "All of our feelings, beliefs, and knowledge are based on our internal thoughts, both conscious and subconscious. We can be positive or negative, enthusiastic; dull, active,or passive. The first step in changing our attitudes is to change our inner conversations." www.marin.cc.ca.us/don/study/2positive.html

Faith: The Basis of Meditation

An act of meditation is actually an act of faith—of faith in your spirit,
in your own potential. Faith is the basis of meditation.
Not of faith in something outside you—a metaphysical Buddha,
an unattainable ideal, or someone else's words.
The faith is in yourself, in your own "Buddha-nature."
You too can be a Buddha,
an awakened being that lives and responds
in a wise, creative, and compassionate way.
~ Martine Batchelor, Meditation for Life

I resonate strongly with these words. I feel faith, I trust love, and I follow my heart. While I respect someone else's words, I never stop listening to my whispering heart. That is the beauty of meditation.[1] This is my choice. What is yours?

Do you trust? Do you believe in yourself? Have you seen the Buddha in the mirror lately? I trust you have! If not, it is never too late. You always have the now!

---

1. "There are 508 studies [of the effects of meditation] collected in Volumes 1 through 5 of *Scientific Research on Maharishi's Transcendental Meditation: Collected Papers.* These studies are listed by volume with annotations that summarize their findings. Each reference also includes previous publication information and/or details of the institutes or universities at which the research was conducted as well as conferences at which the research results were presented. "www.tm.org

Fingerprints

Values are like fingerprints.
Nobody's are the same,
but you leave 'em all over everything you do.
~ Elvis Presley

Be aware of what you say, think and do! Everything is energy and the law of cause and effect is created by this energy. Try to leave fingerprints of love, honesty, kindness, and truth wherever you go. The King made a point, didn't he? No more to say, just space for more contemplation.

Heaven is Full of Answers

A father and son were walking along a sea wall by the beach.
The father was tall enough that he could see over the wall, but the boy was not.
The father described to his son all the
wonders that he saw—the endless water, the waves, the foam, everything.
Finally, the boy asked, "Lift me up father, so I can see too."
This is what you must ask of your spiritual Father.
But YOU must ask it. It must be YOUR request.
~ The Daily Guru

Heaven is full of answers to prayer for which no one bothered to ask.
~ Billy Graham

Heaven = God = Heart = Power Within = Wisdom = Love = The Present Moment = Me = You. Here you'll find the answers. Let us all pray to heaven for more love, more peace, more bliss, and more healing for the world in the service of truth and love.

We are unique and honored! Our choices are valuable and respected by the divine energy of creation. Ask and thou shall receive. Let's ask for healing. Let's ask for people to experience love and for us to believe in love. Do we want to see things happening? The planet healing? Children laughing? Let's begin with ourselves! Let's ask. Let us pray with the deepest devotion of our souls.

SHARING:

Dear friends:

Stop your prayers. Stop asking, stop wishing for and just wait and see. You do not need to be lifted up to see. You need to get your feet back on the ground. There is nothing to pray for, nothing to ask for, and nothing to wish for. Everything *is* what it is. Nothing needs to be changed or improved. You may think there are wrong things going on in the world, but just remember that "right and wrong" are concepts that we have created, just like the concepts of good or bad, fair and unfair, divine and evil, spiritual and shallow.

The universe is unfolding in a certain way and no prayer, no meditation, no wishful thinking, no affirmation, no pledge, no desire, no intention will change this. Stop your judgments about the way things should be. Stop deciding what is acceptable for you and what is not. Stop wishing things were different in the world. Whether you understand it or not, what shall happen, will happen. It is what it is. Open your eyes and see.

Francisco
Mexico

RESPONSE:

Dear Francisco,

Thank you for sharing your truth. It is honored and most appropriate. With your message, four words appear in my mind: The Power of Now.

We all are One.
Ivonne

Honoring God

The ignorant work for their own profit, Arjuna.
The wise work for the welfare of the world, without thought for themselves.
By abstaining from work, you will confuse the ignorant who are engrossed in their
actions.
Perform all work carefully, guided by compassion.
~ Bhagavad-Gita, *3:25-26*

Can any lock keep love confined within
when the loving heart's tiny tears escape and confess it?
The unloving belong only to themselves,
But the loving belong to others to their very bones.
~ Tirukural *8:71-71*

When you are with someone you love very much, you can talk and it is pleasant,
but the reality is not in the conversation.
It is in simply being together.
Meditation is the highest form of prayer.
In it, you are so close to God that you don't need to say a thing—
it is just great to be together.
~ *Swami Chetanananda*

First, I want to say thank you to all of those who choose to take the time to
read the messages from my heart. Today, I am honoring all human beings whose
intentions remain rooted in Love. I wish to honor those who assist people, who
open up to the advice of others, and those who have ears to listen to both the spoken and unspoken messages. I wish to honor those who, with their hearts, plan
their lives, who keep on trusting no matter what, who love existence, love the
planet, love their children, and love their lives. I wish to honor those who play
and work for the sake of truth and love, who are willing to cry, to laugh, to give
no power to the words, "This is not possible." I wish to honor those who dare to
express the words "I love you" to the ones they love and those who are not con-

fined by other people's personal interests and keep on being true to themselves. I wish to honor those who smile, who play, who would not lie for self-gain. I honor those who are learning to be better parents and those who are seeking help. I honor those whose mistakes are taken as a teaching and not as a burden. I honor you all because I honor God.

Love will prevail.

The Power of Love

Try to be reasonable in the way you grow, and don't ever think it is too late.
It is never too late. Even if you are going to die tomorrow,
keep yourself straight and clear and be a happy human being today.
If you keep your situation happy day by day,
you will eventually reach the greatest happiness of enlightenment.
~ *Lama Thubten Yeshe,* The Bliss of Inner Fire

In the year 2002, the Mastery Life volunteers and I attended the "Power of Love" seminar given by Dr. Donald Schnell and his wife, Marilyn Diamond. I was able to witness, not only in others but also in myself, how the transformation of an attitude, perception, or thought can occur powerfully in a positive way through the power of Love.

Everybody at the seminar bonded almost immediately. If it is rare to see that between two people, imagine fifty or more bonding as one. Through different exercises the attendees not only opened their minds to new possibilities, but most importantly, opened their hearts. With basic principles as a major focus—no criticisms, no condemnations, no judgments, and no procrastinating—the seminar was more than we expected. It was an experience of the true transmission of love and the realization that many courageous souls are needed to share, give, teach, and express the power of Love that resides in each of us.

Whoever you are, wherever you live, wherever you work, try bringing the message that love is all that is needed to heal, smile. and live day by day with an open heart, with a happy mind. and a blissful self! Are you willing to share the love that you are? Be a happy human being today. You are truly—we all are—a gift from God as Love.

SHARING:

Dearest Ivonne,

Thank you for everything you do and everything you feel. Thank you for the purity of your intention. Today I thank you for the powerful phrase, "those who work and play for the sake of truth and love." I find this pivotal in understanding human existence. This is the mission of our souls and the reason to live in a physical form—to work and play for the sake of truth and love.

It is so simple to experience but so easy to forget. I ask of God within to remind me when I lose my focus. Maybe all I need is the laughter of my son.

I love you.
Mauricio
Mexico

PART VII
YOU ARE A BUDDHA

I beg your pardon, whom did you say
you were looking for?
Could you describe that person to God?
But do it under your own risk...for her response
is always the same:
You are what you are looking for.
~ Ame

Love is in the Air

It is no longer good enough to cry peace.
We must act peace, live peace, and live in peace.
~ Shenandoah proverb

It is no longer good enough to cry love; we must act love, live love, and live in love. It is time to make things happen. Action is required! It is time to love. It is time to live, to breathe, and to be aware that the moment is here and now. We might have had grand disappointments, we might be experiencing situations that could create the illusion of sadness in our minds, but time keeps moving on. Let's love today. Let's be peaceful today, and let's have the courage to love and celebrate life with the passion that lovers feel for each other. Let's play through work. Let's use our imagination for the creation of a better now.

Dance, smile, share, and celebrate! It's about time! If you want to indulge your energy in forgetting who you are, that's okay, but remember you have a choice—right here, right now. Create action. Just smiling at others makes a difference.

If your cells feel like dancing, let's all create a meditation of love—in the air, in the earth, in the sky, and in your soul. Dance and celebrate!

SHARING:

Dear Ivonne,

A long-time friend ceased all communication with me. She even told people at her office not to receive my calls. Our long-term friendship had begun to evolve into a deeper connection. I don't know what happened. She excused herself by saying she was busy. My question is: Can someone really be afraid of love? Is it possible that someone could close the door to love? What is your experience and what do you think?

Manuel
Argentina

RESPONSE:

Dear Manuel:

I don't feel that someone could be afraid of love. Maybe they could fear the concept of love. Whatever the reaction or response of your friend is just that. It is her choice and her creation. You could focus more on your choice of thoughts—thinking that someone else is afraid to love. Gather your focus and continue loving anyway. Remember that true love always finds a way. Create time to watch the situation.

As for closing the door to love, haven't you heard that love is the most powerful key in the universe? Haven't you heard that there are no doors to love? Just love. Believe me, it always comes back to you!

In service to love,
Ivonne

You are a Holy Being

In the Bible, when Moses approached the burning bush on Mt. Sinai
God told him, "Take off your shoes, for you are standing on holy ground."
The same instruction applies to us: Wherever you stand is holy ground.
Wherever there is life, the ground is holy and life is everywhere.
The question is, are you in it?
~ Alan Cohen

No, it's never the same trip. God is too original to do the same thing twice.
~ Alan Cohen

Isn't this moment that you are reading these words a holy one? Isn't it holy being able to live and to breathe? Isn't the diversity that exists in our creation holy? Isn't the outcome of our manifestations holy? Isn't the possibility of change holy? Isn't the gift to love and be loved, holy? You are holy. Your heart and your capacity to love is a blessing for yourself and others.

Be aware of this. Fear not what others think of you. Fear not your capacity to live and love. Become an opener of doors. Allow your creativity to flow, making unique patterns of light each holy moment of your life. You are the creator of your reality and the power to paint this creation with colors is yours alone. Dare to create your holy moments in an original pattern. Include love, spontaneity, and a willingness to smile. Dare to dance alone, working blissfully.

Call someone you love and haven't told in a long time that you love them.

Write a poem, draw a picture—anything that could serve as a reminder of your power of creation.

Celebrate a holy day without concepts of religion, the do's and don'ts.

You are a very courageous soul. You are love; you are holy. Create a beauty-full you.

SHARING:

Dearest Ivonne,

Motivated by your emails, I've decided to contact all the people that I love and let them know of this love. To my surprise, many did not respond. Others, especially male friends, thought I was flirting with them! Even though I told myself this doesn't matter, it does for my mind! Have you ever had this type of experience? What is it that matters most?

You are all angels of love!
Adriana
Cancun, Mexico

RESPONSE:

Dearest Adriana,

Thank you for your kind words. We are honored to be of service to you. Regarding your question, yes, I have had similar experiences. Just a week ago, when I emailed a beautiful quote to all my friends, I was inspired with more love for all the people that I know. Only one person responded, however. I was very grateful, both for that one and for the others that didn't. Do you know why? Because when I told them that I loved them, it had nothing to do with them. It had to do with my love for them and my desire to let them know! That was my intention and I fulfilled it.

I celebrate your truth and your courage to let the people you love know that you love them. This is what matters most! We are living now, in this moment. We do not know when we will pass away or transcend. Here and now we can love, we can share, and we can speak. This is what matters to me. You can choose now what matters most to you.

In love,
Ivonne

SHARING:

Dear Ivonne,

I have found myself in a repetitive situation in my life. I love to say to my friends, I love you a lot, and the other day a friend of mine said I was flirting with his wife! Truly, I swear I was not. This has happened to me many times. Someone overheard me telling a college professor that I loved them and everybody thought

I wanted to get the best grade in the class! Why does this happen? Shall I just go ahead and control my feelings and stop saying, I love you?

Thanks for listening.
Eduardo
Puerto Vallarta, Mexico

RESPONSE:

Dearest Eduardo:

Why would you like to stop your heart from expressing itself? I can totally relate to your situation. Whenever I love someone, I say it, without any intention of an intimate relationship or wanting something from him or her. I have had experiences like yours. Yet, despite other people's confusion or their comments and gossip, I keep on saying, I love you whenever it feels right in my heart. I don't regret my actions. I just feel love and express it with all my heart. So say, I love you.

Namaste,
Ivonne

Madly in Love

Love the moment, and the energy of that moment
will spread beyond all boundaries.
~ Corita Kent

My love for you goes beyond existence itself.
Some call me crazy, others say I lack something. They are correct.
I lack mind and judgment and I dare to believe in Love.
~ Ivonne Delaflor

Have you ever been in love? Have you ever loved so passionately, so unconditionally that no matter where your beloved is, or with whom he or she is, you delight in the joyful experience of your beloved's mere existence? If you have experienced this love, I am sure that by now you know you have met God face to face.

Being in love with existence, letting your creativity flow, motivating, praising, exalting, celebrating and sharing all that you are, without limitations, with grand respect to whoever encounters your path—that is meeting God. If you have not yet manifested such an experience, would you risk your habitual self to experience it? Would you allow your heart to open and fall in love with the sunset? Would you be willing to not limit your experience of love? Would you like existence to romance you?

I invite you to look at the stars as a gift from existence to you. I invite you to drink water with gratitude, experiencing water by itself. I invite you to smell the flowers in the garden as if they have been sent to you by the person you love the most. Create a romance with existence. Believe in magic, for we live in a magical world, full of wonderful possibilities.

I invite you to participate in the context of love. How many times can you say I love you? How many times can you think of love? How many times during the day can you smile? I invite you to fall in love with love itself. Feel its passion! Believe in it! Take a chance! What can you lose? You are already a winner and you are Love!

SHARING:

Dearest Ivonne,

Thank you so much for your messages. My Englich [sic] is not very good but I dont [sic] care, I read I dont [sic] understand but I feel something that tickles my heart when I read your words.

Gracias,
Roberto
Chihuahua, Mexico

RESPONSE:

My heart is tickling, too.

In service,
Ivonne

Loving without Attachments

We confuse attachment with love. Attachment is concerned with my needs, my happiness, while love is an unselfish attitude, concerned with the needs and happiness of others.
A relationship free of unrealistic grasping is free of disappointment, conflict, jealousy and other problems, and is fertile ground for the growth of wisdom.
~ Kathleen McDonald, How to Meditate

Can you love, really love without any attachment disguised as words or thoughts in your mind like:

> What would they think?
> Am I going to lose him or her?
> This isn't appropriate.
> He makes me happy.
> She makes me feel whole.

Loving free from expectations, loving freely, loving purely—can you do these things? Would you risk dropping your attachments to false security to experience unconditional love?

> Can you love your children like that?
> Can you love your beloved like that?

Once I told a friend that even though sometimes I was not in the physical presence of my beloved husband, I was content and happy for his existence, without the need to cling to him or to despair because I was not with him in a certain moment. My acquaintance said, "No, that is just a way of evading yourself." Of course, I honored his choice of words, but I did not get attached to his way of thinking.

Have you ever been told how you are "supposed" to feel?
Have you ever been told what you "should" be feeling?
Are you attached to the opinions of others and their expectations of you?
Do you think your happiness depends on your beloved?

Do you think your bliss depends on how much money you have?

Do you think your power depends on how many books you sell or how popular you are?

The experience of detachment includes humbleness, courage, and trust. Leap! Detach yourself from the habit of attachment.

For one week, every night say to yourself:

> *I detach from my attachment to things, people, and situations.*
> *I am free.*
> *I love freely.*
> *I am happy because I am me.*
> *I love my beloved because it is my choice.*
> *I am grateful for the presence of my loved ones.*
> *It is time to love!*

Lift Yourself in Love

"As long as the sun and moon shine in the sky,"
Krishna sang to Radha, "Your name shall be chanted with mine.
And as long as the rivers flow on earth, our love will endure."
~ Krishna speaks to Radha

Dedicated to Marla, who passed away in the year 2002.

Lord Krishna's love for Radha is a beautiful reminder of the miracle of being with someone you love, of sharing, of evolving and growing together. It also speaks of eternity and of unconditional love. This love is experienced and manifested as a sacred and divine relationship with intention. It is a love that assists us in growing and evolving in the most celebratory and positive ways. This love is available for everyone. It is who we are!

Many people are confused about love. They confuse it with attachment, with the fear of losing someone or something, and with expectations. Often love is confused with demands from others of what to do or be, how to behave or act. I ask you now, is this love? What if your grandest experience of love in a relationship only lasted for one day or only one hour? Would you be grateful? Would you cling to the illusion that it must last forever? What is forever in romance? Is it an attachment? Could forever be just a sacred moment?

If you have experienced, even for one moment, the presence of a soulmate in your life I believe that you have experienced the Soulmate called God. Perhaps you have had the experience of "falling" (or lifting) in love, or feeling butterflies in your stomach. Have you had the experience of looking into someone's eyes and seeing eternity? I have had that experience. I have fallen in love with God. I have loved and surely, I will love many beautiful beings as my own heart and self. The gift of being able to love or be in love, even for one single moment, is the eternity that lovers and beloveds speak about.

If you still have not manifested the experience of falling (lifting) in love with love itself, relax and focus on lowering your expectations. Remember the good things that have happened in your life. Remember the sweet beings that have smiled at you. Look at the sunset, smell a flower—those are gifts for you from the Divine, from existence, from God. You are being romanced constantly. It is up to you to choose to see it and experience it.

Lift yourself in love. Fall in love with love itself, for as Krishna said, "...as long as the rivers flow on earth, our love will endure."

Love Now

Let this be my last word,
that I trust in Your Love.
~ Rabindranath Tagore

The morning light has flooded my eyes.
This is Your message to my heart.
Your face is bent from above; Your eyes look down on my eyes,
and my heart has touched Your feet.
~ Rabindranath Tagore

A woman asked me, "How is it possible to feel passion for something that is not human? How can you be in love or feel in love just because you see a sunset? The only way to be in love is if someone else from the opposite sex romances you. It is impossible to be and feel in love just because we are alive."

I replied: "When your beloved gives you a flower, you feel appreciated and romanced, right?"

She said, "Yes."

"When your beloved invites you to have dinner in a nice restaurant, you are excited and like to dress up, right?"

She said, "Yes."

"When your beloved tells you, I love you, you think he is in love with you, right?"

She said, "Yes!"

"When your beloved doesn't say I love you, you begin to ask why, right?"

She said, "Yes."

Then I asked her, "Have you noticed the flowers in your garden? Their fragrance is free for you to smell. Have you noticed the palm trees moving with the wind? If your eyes watch, they will dance. Have you noticed that the sunset is different every day for your eyes to see? Its colors delight and warm your heart. Have you noticed that you are able to love? Loving is truly empowering for you. Have you noticed that existence is in love with you?"

To those questions she answered, "No, not until now," then she began to cry.

Now is a good day to start to love. The experience of love from your own heart for yourself is truly a miracle. I constantly remind myself of this by contemplating death. I know that people die and I know that one day my body will die. That is the only thing I know for sure. This thought gives me a choice when I forget the passionate Love of creation—the choice of loving or not loving, of seeing everything as the miracle it is or not, of enjoying the beings I love or not. Don't wait to love. Speak to those that you love. Share your love. This is what I call the "Romance with Existence."

Trust that if you say "I love you" to someone, it will create ripples of love for you! Expecting to receive back the love you give limits the experience of "Romance with the Divine." Do not be afraid of love. Love knows no fear. Love will permeate every cell of your being, if you just allow it to.

I invite you to find the beauty and truth that you are by witnessing and contemplating simple things. Remember that all experiences are appropriate. All is love. It is okay to choose to be sad, happy, angry, focused—whatever your choice is. It is appropriate to be who you want to be.

SHARING:

Dear Ivonne,

Throughout my life, I have been a student of the mind, always studying about evolution and consciousness. I have been blessed with a beautiful family. I have been married three times. I have a nice relationship with my ex-wives and cannot complain about anything. My third wife appeared in my life like a playful angel. It took courage for me to say yes to the experience of welcoming my soulmate, which I thought I had found before, but never realized that it was a concept of my mind. I am here now, loving her, loving myself and feeling free for the first time in my life.

When you speak about being in love with life, it is so true. I haven't found that in books, but in the eyes of my wife. I have not found it by going to workshops, but by swimming in the ocean. I have not found it in demonstrating my truth, but in my silence. I have not found it in many people, but I have in the transmission of your words. My wife Adriana and I are most grateful.

Raul
Mexico

RESPONSE:

Dear Raul,

Thank you, thank you, thank you. We are in love with Love. I feel humbled by your words.

With love,
Ivonne

Peace within is the Only Way

All tremble when there is a weapon,
Everyone fears death;
Feeling for others as for oneself,
One should neither kill nor cause to kill.
~ The Dhammapada

The purpose of all the major religious traditions
is not to construct big temples on the outside,
but to create temples of goodness and compassion inside, in our hearts.
~ *His Holiness the Dalai Lama,* The Good Heart

When the war in Iraq began we received more than 250 email messages in one day speaking about war and how to react or act against it. I also heard many people saying, "We must stop the war in Iraq! Send your letters to Congress!"

I heard many people choosing to complain, cry, worry, and panic. Although intentions to stop the war might be wonderful and good, what are we really doing to create this?

We must start peace within ourselves! How do we expect to make a change if we don't nurture our inner world first? We want war to cease, but we keep on fighting with the ones we love—with our own family. We want love, we want to save the world and to be the light that guides everyone and everything, but we judge people and have no love for others in our lives. We want hunger to stop, but our desires for material manifestation, fame, or recognition grow as fast as hunger does. We want people to love us, but we keep on setting our priorities in wanting and desiring new things. We want our children to be happy, but we keep feeding our minds with negative news, judgmental thoughts, and criticisms.

I invite you to vote for peace in the world—but in your inner world first! Have fun, work while you play, and play while you work. Love. Set your priorities straight, yet do not take for granted those whom love you. Forget excuses like, I can't, I have no luck, I have no time, I am busy. Treat yourself with kindness and respect and the rest will follow. Continue to love.

I vote for peace…inner peace. I vote for love. I vote for kindness. I vote for you. As His Holiness the Dalai Lama says, "Create a temple of compassion inside your heart!" Let's feed each other with good news for our minds. Cease the war within yourself and watch the miracles that will manifest in your life and in the rest of the world.

PART VIII
MESSAGES YOU ALREADY KNOW

All divine wisdom emanates from within your soul.
You have a treasure to discover quietly inside yourself.
No books, striving or searching will deliver
what you already have inside.
Instead of buying so many things
to "become" enlightened,
why not save some money and use what is already inside the library of your heart?
~ Ivonne Delaflor

Open Your Heart

If we divide into two camps and stand in one camp while attacking the other,
the world will never have peace.
We will always blame and condemn those we feel are responsible for wars
and social injustice,
without recognizing the degree of violence within ourselves.
We must work on ourselves and with those we condemn
if we want to have a real impact.
~ *Ayya Khema,* Be An Island

What are your priorities in life? What role does love play in your world? It saddens me to see the wounded children in Iraq. It saddens me to know that even without war there are children all over the world suffering, being abused, disrespected, and denied the experience of the joy of childhood. It saddens me to see people using non-peaceful ways to try to create peace. It saddens me to see how judgment and control give importance to priorities that will vanish when the human form dies. Nevertheless, it strengthens my belief in love, in its power, and in the faith that truth and peace shall prevail.

The children in the world deserve to live their lives surrounded by love, not pain. They deserve to play with dolls not guns. They deserve to laugh freely, not to be shot at by soldiers. They deserve to hug their parents, not be separated from them.

Please open your heart and believe for one moment that you can really change the world. Do not judge or use harsh words towards those who are not choosing peace. Think love, send love, vibrate as love.

I am no Mother Teresa, nor am I another Gandhi, but I do have two wonderful children that laugh, cry, and play. In the oneness that we all are, they remind me how beautiful and precious life is and how absurd it is to judge or fight one another. I want the children of the world to experience being human as the most magical experience of their lives!

I've heard many people on the spiritual path say, "Everything is just as it should be. This is what is happening. We must observe and watch." I agree with some aspects of this and I do observe and watch, but I also use my free will to choose love. My human heart, my awareness as a mother cannot help but feel the need to do something to assist the children of the world to live in love.

> Will you believe?
> Will you pray?
> Will you dare to choose love?
> It brings me joy to believe in you!

God Speaks through Me

Before you speak, ask yourself, is it kind, is it necessary, is it true?
Does it improve on the silence?
~ Sai Baba

I invite you to do an experiment for one week. Before you speak with someone have this thought in mind, "God, speak through me." (If you don't like the word God you can choose the word Love, Joy, or Kindness.) Please keep the focus and intention very positive and loving. After repeating this to yourself, start speaking to others. Watch your choice of words. What energy vibrates within you? Are you more patient? More kind? Less judgmental?

I ask God now to write through me, and what comes is, "Stay in the moment. Love, breathe, trust, choose, laugh, respect, uplift, share, admire, praise, accept, let go, dance, celebrate, smile."

I honor you and delight in the Divine opportunity to be One with you all.

Enlightenment is for Everyone

Illness is not cured by saying the word "medicine," but by taking medicine.
Enlightenment is not achieved by repeating the word "God,"
but by directly experiencing God.
~ Sankara

I was listening to a person talking about enlightenment. This person explained that enlightenment belonged only to those who are celibate, who are not in an intimate relationship, and who meditate for a minimum of eight hours a day. After hearing this conversation, I found this quote from the book, *Zen Master Hakuin*:

> Even if you are a monk, if your practice of the Way is not intense,
> If your aspiration is not pure, how are you any different from a layman?
> Again, even if you are a layman, if your aspiration is intense and your conduct wise, Why is this any different from being a monk?

What is enlightenment anyway, but the state of peace and grace that is generated by the intention of a pure heart to love, love and love more? Enlightenment is for everyone! You don't need to be a monk to be enlightened. You just need to create happy thoughts, never harm anyone, trust in peace, and follow your heart. It is as simple and enlightening as that!

Living beyond Labels

There is exalted greatness in everything small.
~ *Kook,* Orot HaKodesh

Jelaluddin Rumi (a well-known Sufi teacher and perhaps the greatest mystical poet of all times) was in despair. His teacher had gone to another village without telling him. Rumi yearned for the presence of his teacher, Shams-i-Tabriz, an enlightened being dressed as a beggar. Shams had the purest of wisdom that comes not from scholarly certifications, but from the highest realm itself—the realm of the heart.

Rumi sent one of his students to look for his beloved Shams. The student finally found him inside a tavern sharing beer with a young man, talking about the mysteries and beauty of life. The young man he was with was called Francis. (Later in his life, Francis would live in the town of Assisi.)

You never know what your teachers will look like in this lifetime. We all serve both as teachers and as disciples to one another. We are eternal students of life itself, of nature, of the Divine. We are all on the human journey. We are sourcing the moment, learning from our mistakes and striving for a life of fulfillment, joy, and peace. Whatever the form, belief, or situation we choose to create, we all are on the journey.

These days so many individuals find themselves confused regarding the teacher-disciple relationship. This is true not only for those who are looking for teachers but also for the teachers themselves. Marketing strategies to sell "their" wisdom are being used and abused. This is not a judgment; it is simply the way it is.

Shams was there when Rumi realized their heart connection. Rumi looked directly into Shams' eyes and said, "What I thought before as God, today I experienced through a human being." Touched by love, Rumi immediately abandoned his life at the dervish's feet.

How could a beggar be an enlightened one? Would we have the eyes to see an enlightened one if she appeared right now? How often do we miss the Buddha because we are distracted by marketing, labels, appearance, intellect, and more?

Some of us have been on the guru roller coaster—disciple, teacher, and all those labels that serve as a focus for the mind to choose higher and more lovable situations. We have met wonderful people. Some of them pretend perfection, which, at times, we have all done. Some of them praise the qualities of human beings without practicing what they say. Some are as simple and innocent as a child and yet powerfully connected to the Divine. Some are very honest and truthful beings. All are part of this game call living.

At Mastery Life, we have a commitment to serve, assist, and love as much as possible. We all are in the Mastery of Life, learning, experiencing, choosing, and sourcing different manifestations on our paths. We are focusing on seeing beyond the labels created by the mind, society, and spiritual beliefs. Labels have no value except the ones we choose to place upon them. The energy beyond the label, which could be a spiritual name, surname, or organizational name is what really makes an impact.

Someone shared with us that he was given a sannyasin name by his guru. One day, the guru was very upset because his student forgot to bow down, so he took away the man's sannyasin "label." How can someone, who named you a sannyasin, project his own emotional process on you and decide to remove the "title" he had already given you? Labels, and the attachment the mind has to them are unnecessary when it comes to love.

The higher intelligence of the universe is always at work even when we are unaware of it. To repeat from our hearts what we have said many times, *enlightenment is for everyone* and is found in the present moment, not in the future. There are no workshops that will deliver the state of self-realization. Self-realization is a process of rediscovering oneself, and it begins in the moment with the simplest things of life, surrendering to the present by letting go of the desire to be right, to control, to manipulate, to have our way. Accepting and bringing more love into your life and situations is real. This costs nothing. It is totally free.

Shams did not charge Rumi for his wisdom or his time. We believe that people who have this spiritual, emotional, and mental understanding have a divine responsibility to assist others in finding their own mastery. It is here, now. However, it is important to be cautious of owning someone else's process. Don't say, "Because of me you are happier. Because of me, you have succeeded. If you don't want to pay my expensive rates for my wisdom, then you cannot be enlightened!"

The day is so short. We don't have time to put on our spiritual ego medals to show off our apparent "accomplishments." The higher power works through all of us. Look at the flowers. Are they saying, "Because of me, you can experience exotic fragrances"? Does the rain say, "Because of me you have vegetables that grow and can nourish you"? No. Everything is as it should be. Everything has its mission. Nature is the grandest teacher of all.

Who is a real monk? One who shaves his head and lives in a cave?

Who is a real Christian? One who goes to mass every Sunday?

Who is a real swami? One who wears orange robes and chants in Sanskrit?

The real monk is the one who is guided by compassion and love toward all beings.

The real Christian listens to the teachings of Jesus and applies the message of love in her everyday life.

The real swami has affirmed life and serves with the true richness of hers/his heart without attachment to acknowledgement or praise of his selfless service.

There is a well-known saying:

Do not follow Jesus, become a Jesus.

Do not follow Buddha, become a Buddha.

Do not follow God, become a God.

If we may add something to this quote:

You already are Jesus, Buddha, and God. Just remember, breathe and choose love, no matter what the situation is, what words have been said, and what confusion exists. Choose love and in stillness find the real power, the subtle aspect, the power of Love.

Stay in the moment. Enjoy the beings around you. Make the most of this very moment. It is the one and only moment. Enjoy it and celebrate it; live it as the life that you are!

SHARING OF THE MONTH

The Mastery Life Team[1] would like to share one of the poems that the founder of the Mastery of Life Organization wrote a couple of months ago. It was awarded the Editor's Choice Award for Outstanding Poetry presented by the International Library of Poetry. The intention of our sharing is not the recogni-

---

1.   All the volunteers that donate their time, wisdom and knowledge to Mastery Life, a non-profit organization in Cancun, Mexico, represent the Mastery Life Team. They have attended various workshops and training seminars to guide others with humbleness, compassion and love. www.masterylife.com

tion of the award itself, which we volunteers of Mastery Life are very proud of, but for the message of peace that this simple poem has beyond the written words. We hope you enjoy it and that you can begin smiling more each day.

Your friends,
The volunteers of Mastery Life

> JUST A SMILE
> Written by Ivonne Delaflor
>
> *Dedicated to the inner child of all human beings.*
>
> If I close my eyes, would the world disappear
> With the concept of war that creates so much fear?
> If I open my eyes after that shall I see…
> All the children of earth smiling at me?
> It is the hope in my heart that prays now
> For the soaring eagle of courage to fly.
> And carry in its wings a message for peace
> While the dream vanishes and reality appears.
> Just a smile in all times is required
> For a miracle of healing to occur.
> With the faith that the world will assist
> All those brave crusaders of love.
> It is the Power of Love that will free
> All the minds trapped in selfish journeys.
> And for those beings who can still believe
> The universe will assist them with its blessings.
> Just a Smile…

SHARING:

Dearest Ivonne,

I was at a cyber café the other day and I happened to look at my neighbor's computer. There was a message from you that said, "The Grandest Miracle of the Millennium." My body, my heart, everything melted with that idea! Thank you so much. Wherever this idea was inspired, I sense it had to do with God. Do you give workshops for children outside Cancun?

Would you come to Bolivia?

God bless you.
Diana
Bolivia

RESPONSE:

Dear Diana,

Thank you so much. I feel humbled and full of joy for your words. I wrote that message with my heart and my belief in peace and the children of our planet! Yes, God inspired it. I consider myself in service to this Divine power.

Regarding a workshop in Bolivia, not yet, but perhaps in the near future. You never know (and neither do I).

Love from God,
Ivonne

Sacred Space within Relationships

First keep the peace within yourself, then you can also bring peace to others.
~ Thomas à Kempis

Think of all the beauty still left around you and be happy.
~ Anne Frank

Space. I begin with this five-letter word that implies enormity and also confusion. When it comes to relationships, this small word either creates great help or grand disharmony. More and more frequently women and men are not only requesting but also demanding "their own space." Space to be alone. Space to do the things they like, to rest from the madness of work, family tensions or the blessed parenting world, which is a 24-hour-a-day intensive training. Even when children are sleeping, somehow parents still think about their child's world until they themselves finally go to sleep. Others, with or without children, may continue to think about work even when they are finished for the day. We carry all that we do in our minds even when we are not doing it. We have parenting, work, plans, colleagues, worries, dreams, expectations, and so on, in our heads. With our minds so full of thoughts, judgments, comparisons, and much more, we clamor for space.

Space is very sacred. Children need their own space to play, a healthy space or environment (whatever you choose to call it) for growth. Men need space to work, to accomplish, to manifest, to materialize their power and their preferences in a positive way. Women need space to create, to be, to feel useful, creative, worthwhile, and to relax from a full day of mothering or work or both. Like plants, we all need space to grow.

When it comes to relationships, do we allow enough space for togetherness to grow? Do we manifest an harmonious environment to share and delight with someone else, within the same shared environment that is respectful, loving, and celebratory? Can we offer a space that celebrates others for their growth, endurance and strength? What about a space to be and live joyfully in even when we are not physically alone? Can we create a space that welcomes differences as gifts rather than as problems or things we must change to please another?

A friend of mine said, "Thank God we are all different!" He is so right. True space is manifested when we embrace the diversity, respecting others, their likings, the things that motivate them to grow and be happy. This doesn't mean that you must sacrifice your own likings for someone else's, for in that case the balance would be lost. True space is based on respect and support. We might not agree with someone else's beliefs, but we can understand that it is their own choice and their own liking. *Respect* is not separate from *space*.

Self-space can be created anywhere. When we realize that the moment is as it is, and when we choose to create that moment with the grandest vision possible, then all and everyone included in that space becomes a joy, a learning process and a mirror of opportunities to grow more.

Be aware of how you use the word space. It is a good word and with awareness, it is a better one. When it comes to relationships, it is important to share space and learn together in that space. We are responsible for our creations, whatever they look like—job, family issues, child raising, marital situations. We might not be able to change a situation, but we can always change the way we choose to see it. We can choose to see it as a situation lacking space or one that is full of space, enabling evolution and growth. Create the space for you to realize that there is nowhere to go, nowhere to hide from the things that disturb you. Let us assume our responsibilities.

Space is not only about how the furniture is arranged in your home. Space goes beyond that. It is the simple recognition that in this time, moment and momentum, space itself is a blessing to grow, share, and make the most of. It is not about having a clean and orderly home, but also about having order in the mind to be grateful for relationships, for challenges, for opportunities that manifest to grow and to keep on choosing to love.

Have you ever heard of a rose growing in the same piece of land with a dozen or more roses saying, "Excuse me, I need my own space"? I know this is an extreme example, but truly, the clearer we are in our minds and the more we set priorities, the more self-space we will have to create the space everyone is talking about.

Create a space of celebration, of acknowledgment, of love. What else do we need? The day we die, we will have a lot of space and no time to think about what we want. Today we are alive. Today we are breathing. Let us create a space of love. Space cannot be demanded; it creates itself. I believe there is no better space than the one that is shared with someone you love.

SHARING:

Dear Ivonne,

I love to run. I run marathons every time I am invited to. I am not the best runner, but I feel like I am sometimes. Nevertheless, my friends and family, who probably don't do much exercise, continuously say that I am running to feel important. They criticize that I am doing it to attract attention and that I have no chance of winning. I have tried to tell them that I simply love running! I do it when the timing is appropriate, when my children are well cared for. I mean, I don't run every day. This may sound silly to you, but it is annoying that my best friends and family and all those who don't exercise at all, keep on telling me this. I've tried to tell them using many different words, but I have come to realize that they don't really want to listen to how I feel about running. It is so annoying.

Has something like this ever happened to you? If this is silly, just disregard this message and I will understand. Also, can you recommend a spiritual teacher and retreat for me to attend? Thank you for your newsletters. They are wonderful tools to keep me focused on choosing the positive in life.

Ana Paula
Brasil

RESPONSE:

Dear Ana Paula,

Know that anything that is important to you is not at all silly. Yes, I have experienced events like that, many more times than you think! I listen but also always contemplate who and where is it coming from. Often, fellow human beings without a creative focus find sport in complaining or projecting their limitations onto someone else. This is not a judgment, rather an acknowledgement of seeing that human nature sometimes works like that. For example, I love writing. I don't write just because I have a newsletter that many wonderful people like you have signed up for. To be honest, I do it to keep my mind clear, emptying as much as I can from daily pressures and activities so I can focus. For me, writing is a meditation and a way of processing my words and thoughts into the best possible medium. Sometimes I achieve that, sometimes I don't, but it's still a good way to clear my mind, to embrace a new day with more optimism and a positive attitude.

Keep on running and enjoy what you do. Ask yourself what is really bothering you. Is it what they say or what you think they should be saying? Whatever the reason, run with clarity. Speak your truth. The truth is powerful when expressed with kindness, compassion and love. We all are Mastering Life. All of us—teachers, scientists, presidents, mothers, fathers, gurus, all and everyone are Mastering Life. It has been said by mystics and sages of all times that you can't stop the waves, (there will always be waves—sometimes big, sometimes small) but you can always learn how to surf.

Generally, I do not particularly recommend people to go and see teachers or gurus. I think each person needs to find his or her own way. However, I am happy to recommend someone with a 100 percent positive focus that I have had the privilege to meet. He maintains the positive on the higher frequencies and guides in very humble ways to recognize that the greatest teacher comes from within. His name is Alan Cohen.[1]

All love and positive thoughts for you,
Ivonne

SHARING:

Dear Ivonne,

What are the two best pieces of advice you have ever received, and would you share them with me? This is a question I've wanted to ask you for a long time. Hope to see you soon and please keep me updated with the development of the intentional community.

Besos,
Adriana
Mexico

RESPONSE:

Dear Adriana,

Great to hear from you! Wow! I have received much valuable advice from many extraordinary beings but I will share with you the two statements that I will never forget and always have in mind.

---

1. Mr. Alan Cohen wrote the foreword for this book *Mastering Life* and is also a recognized spiritual teacher worldwide. Author of *Mr. Everit's Secret, The Dragon Doesn't Live Here Anymore* and many more. www.alancohen.com

Maria Purpura once told me: "People will always tell you what to do, what you should change, and they will offer their suggestions about mothering and everything, but the best advice I can give you is for you to always follow your heart."

Mr. Chick Moorman's advice was: "When you go and give workshops, always have fun." Hope this serves your purpose.

Ivonne

Peace

Music to hear, why hear'st thou music sadly?
Sweets with sweets war not, joy delights in joy.
~ Shakespeare

Real generosity is doing something nice for someone who will never find out.
~ Frank A. Clark

In the year 2002, I heard many people asking questions and making statements like, "When will there be war?" "Do you think everyone is already prepared with a gas mask?" "There is nothing we can do to make a change occur." "War is a business. War is normal."

Do you really feel powerless to make a change? For me, what is real is Love. War is not normal. Normal for me is peace.

Have you noticed that military clothes are fashionable again these days and people love it! I am amazed at the marketing of war. I've heard people say they believe that war is a solution that war is necessary, that war will bring security, and that war is not against people but governments—those are the people whose ordinary life is at war. They live a mental war, judging others, hating, abusing, and deceiving. The choice of attitudes that people who defend war decide to make part of their lives amazes me,

It saddens me to see how good people are controlled not only by governments, ideals, and beliefs, but also by their own minds. If you want love, you give love. If you want to be treated with respect, respect yourself. If you want people to be kind to you, then demonstrate kindness to others. If you are sending hatred and expecting love in return, then that is the war that everybody is talking about.

I invite you to do one good thing for another fellow human being without his or her knowledge. Let's create an energy of giving, without expecting to receive anything in return. Let's say, "Thank you" without expecting to hear, "You're welcome." Let's give love, giving the Source of fulfillment from our hearts. The time has come to love more!

SHARING:

Dearest Ivonne,

I have a spiritual teacher and it seems to me that my closeness to her is making other people uncomfortable. Should one keep her distance from an enlightened being? Should one be not too close to a spiritual guide? My teacher perceived that many were uncomfortable and now she speaks less to me.

Maria
Puerto Rico

RESPONSE:

Dearest Maria:

As Shakespeare says, "Joy delights in joy" and so enlightenment delights in enlightenment. If you are close to your teacher, who you consider enlightened, that reflects your own enlightenment. I believe that once a pure spiritual connection has been made with one's teacher, there is no such concept as being too close or too far. Words said or not said are nothing compared to the feeling of love or purity of that connection.

Should one keep their distance from an enlightened one? Well, only if you are afraid of your own enlightenment! (Forgive my joke.) About your teacher's choice to remain silent, I believe that perhaps that is just your interpretation. If she speaks less with her words that doesn't mean she speaks less with her heart. The voice of the heart is also silent. Silence is a beautiful melody that brings us an opportunity to listen the voice of our own heart.

In the service of Love and light,
Ivonne

The Only Thing You Need

The illusion that we need to awaken from is the world of the thinking mind,
which includes all our spiritual knowledge and concepts.
Even the spiritual path will ultimately prove to be an illusion.
Just focus on what is here now.
If you can see it, hear it, feel it, taste it or smell it, you can focus on it.
To focus on that which is actually here now (present) with you
will bring you into the truth of life.
The tree or the flower in front of you has more power to bring you present
than all the books in the world and all the teachers who have ever existed.
All you have to do is bring yourself present with that which is present.
~ The Daily Guru

One by one, the images of reality as we know it will shatter in the realm of the mind. There are times on this planet to recognize the opportunity of change, transformation, creation, and love. Why would someone try to avoid the reality of who he or she is? Why are negative choices constantly being selected through eons of time? Simply because without the opposite, how can you experience and choose the reality of who you are? Remember that your history has nothing to do with who you already are. The light you emanate is the essence and Source of existence and this shall forever be the experience.

The mind is a tool you must master. In the meantime, do not forget the heart. Many beings, including the ones choosing an alternative spiritual lifestyle, will be challenged by this. Allow the heart to unfold. Remember you are love and as the one and only choice of your highest possibility, rest in the love you choose to be. With practice, you might create a very focused mind but what about the heart? Yes, enlighten the mind and then what? Who do you want to be in this moment? How are you creating the reality you are living? Challenging times are opportunities to transcend and transform oneself into more love.

Remember your choices. Enlightenment is not only meant for the sage that lives in the cave. If you can master your life in the "ordinary" world, if you can choose to keep on creating love wherever you go, then your enlightenment is imminent. If you are a sage in a cave who is experiencing enlightenment in the mind, share it with the diversity of who you are. Be aware that the "illusion" of distractions can also be a place to hide, even for the enlightened ones. Saying, "I don't want distractions" is a limitation as well as a distraction.

Follow the truth of who you are, the unspoken, the real. All experiences are appropriate and the opportunity of love is everywhere. Just remain being you, which is the experience happening here and now. You do not need seclusion or caves. Just go inward to the sacredness of your heart! Your heart is a great ashram to go to and experience your own illumination, your wholeness, your truth.

Words, words and words, how many words are you able to say? How many words do you need to promise? How many words reflect what you really do? Saying and doing, fulfillment of promises—how many times have you promised yourself something? How many times have you forgotten your promise? Choices again manifesting one by one.

If you were to let go and surrender the choice unto existence, then it will be choiceless, just like a child, free and joyful. A child falls and then stands and a smile comes quickly back onto his face. Without choosing, a child experiences existence freely, lovingly and playfully. As you grow, your choices begin to manifest for you to be responsible for your creation and experience yourself in all your possibilities.

Know again that your choices create ripples and they have an impact on your creation and your surroundings. Be aware of the words you use. Know that what you experience is what you experience. No one is to blame or to be praised. You create your reality. When you include love in your choices, inevitably more love will come back to you. Be aware that just as *you* choose, others also have that possibility. If you go on promising and promising without fulfilling, it is okay for others to forgive you or not, to understand you or not. It will be their choice. Your creation creates ripples. Remember, all you give comes back to you in one form or another in order for you to keep on choosing what you want to create.

Why are you choosing what you are choosing now?

Do you choose to be with the one you love or do you judge and reject that person?

Do you choose to be healthy in your food decisions and your thoughts?

Do you choose to cling to the past or the future?

Do you choose to be present?

Do you choose to experience freedom or burdens?

Do you choose courage or fear?

Do you choose comparison or acceptance?

Whatever you choose is creating the present reality for you. Whatever your choice, whatever the experience, know that there is always the possibility of choosing again to change your reality.

How many words that you choose to say reflect your actions and thoughts? Can you choose to set yourself some healthy limits? Can you choose more love? Can you choose more Positive Thinking? Can you see that all that is, is you? You just need to choose.

SHARING:

The true Mastering of Life begins with a loving spirit, a willingness to serve and love all as the reflection of the Divine herself. The power of humbleness guides those who are willing to give no matter who or what. Those with pure hearts, pure giving, and pure intentions might threaten the ego of another, including so-called spiritual teachers. On the other hand, these rare souls should continue with their mission. It is a mission to laugh, to dance and uplift all around with the divine example of generosity, open arms and childlike love. Thus, it is said that the kingdom of heaven belongs to all children.

There is no grander master than the love that resides in each human being. All is known; the unknown is within as well. The polarities and the universal laws merge as One, bringing all to a grand era of happiness and sweet bliss. Oneness, cooperation, feminine and masculine, cause and effect are indeed universal truths that serve as guidelines for the new Aquarian era, for the continuation of Mastering Life. It is indeed he-she who will experience the present moment as the only moment ever, the one who will be called a true master, a true guru. For he-she, detached from any needs and desires, while embracing the grand manifestation of energy in all its forms, will heal all in its way with a simple task of love.

So be it and may your choices always be blessed. As above, so below. Blessings for thy Mastering of Life.

Ame

PART IX

CONCLUSION, ONLY FOR NOW

Mastering Life is an eternal game;
the player makes choices on how to play it.
Discovering always that there are no winners or losers,
for this game is as unique as each human breath.
It is as miraculous as the birthing sunrise of a new day.
~ Ivonne Delaflor

Conclusion, Only for Now

Seconds tick you closer to death.
Moments bring you closer to life.
~ Alan Cohen

Dear Reader:

More than three years have passed since we began the journey of this book. I say we because you also have been a part of its creation. Ordinary people with normal everyday human thoughts and insights have authored this unique undertaking. While published books, marketing, and media all direct the reader to the specialist, to the ever-enlightened perfect master, to the living avatars, to celebrities with a passion, to the president or past presidents of this country, this book shares the enlightening wisdom of ordinary people. Through their daily activities they demonstrate the divine qualities of an enlightened being in the journey of Mastering Life.

What about the Buddha in the kitchen? What about the sage on the hospital staff? What about the enlightened delivery driver? What about the patient young urban teacher? What about the master clerk at the hardware store? What about the practice of the rural midwife? These are everyday people living a human life. They are doing the best they can to manifest peace and joy in their lives and the lives of others. Their wisdom may not come from reading or meditating but from their experience of life.

Many people shared their wisdom to bring about this book. Many individuals with different backgrounds, religions and beliefs offered their wise words. Many people wrote to us agreeing, disagreeing, sharing longings, breakthroughs, hopes and fears. Those writers assisted us in bonding with each other in subtle and loving ways. All and everyone came together united in love, not just one teacher offering their words with the ultimate key to success or happiness. We welcome the oneness in diversity to learn, share and continue on this human journey in the best way we can.

It is evident in the comments and the sharing from refreshing human experiences that we are all working on Love. A mother is trying to be more conscious; a father wants to evolve more through his work; a doctor is trying to bring greater health to his patients. The unique qualities of this book can be seen and experienced through what has been written and at the same time the message is beyond the words: Love is what humankind is united by. Love is what makes and will make this world a better place.

If you would like to be involved and offer your assistance to Mastery Life in order to co-create a reality of love for all, you can subscribe to our free newsletter at www.masterylife.com or email me at idelaflor@masterylife.com and share with us your real-life experiences. Tell us about your hopes and fears and what is assisting you to live a life based in peace, harmony and joy. Tell us about your struggles, failures and pain because those are real, too. Let us know if you would like your sharing to be included in the second book we are currently preparing. Through your words we all learn and the opportunity to serve others emerges to fuel a life based in trust rather than fear and to choose Mastery in whatever we do.

In the name of our collective consciousness, I offer my gratitude to you with all my heart and celebrate with you our journey of Mastery, our journey of dreams, our journey of being human and our journey of love.

Until the next book, remember to bring Mastery to your Life through Love.

Ivonne Delaflor
September 2004

RESOURCES

SUGGESTED WEBSITES

Chick Moorman www.chickmoorman.com

Thomas Haller www.thomashaller.com

Alan Cohen www.alancohen.com

Synchronicity Foundation International www.synchronicity.org

Alex Slucki www.huellasdeluz.com

The Soulmate Called God www.soulmatecalledgod.com

Translations from the Heart www.insighttrans.com

The Power of Love Foundation www.spiritualjava.com

Kirtan Chanting www.jaiuttal.com

Breath Mastery www.breathmastery.com

The Daily Guru www.TheDailyGuru.com

Conscious One www.consciousone.com

Swami Savita www.swamisavita.com

BEBA Organization www.beba.org

SUGGESTED BOOKS

Barks, Coleman. *Rumi: The Book of Love—Poems of Ecstasy and Longing; The Soul of Rumi: A New Collection of Ecstatic Poems; The Illuminated Rumi.*

Byron, Thomas. *Dhammapada* (Shambhala Pocket Classic).

Cohen, Alan. *Why Your Life Sucks (And What You Can Do About It); The Dragon Doesn't Live Here Anymore: Loving Fully, Living Freely; Dare to Be Yourself: How to Quit Being An Extra in Other People's Movies and Become the Star of*

Your Own; I Had It All the Time: When Self-Improvement Gives Way to Ecstasy.

Green, Brian. *The Elegant Universe: Superstrings, Hidden Dimensions and the Quest for the Ultimate Theory.*

Hawkins, David R. *Power vs. Force: The Hidden Determinants of Human Behavior.*

Hendricks, Gay and Kate Ludeman. *The Corporate Mystic: A Guidebook for Visionaries With Their Feet On the Ground.*

King, Karen L. *The Gospel of Mary of Magdala: Jesus and the First Woman Apostle.*

Klein, Allen. *The Change-Your-Life Quote Book.*

Lao Tsu, Gia-Fu Feng and Jane English (Translators). *Tao Te Ching: 25th Anniversary Edition.*

Moorman, Chick. *Talk Sense To Yourself: Language and Person Power.*

Rumi, Jelalludin and John Moyne, A.J. Arberry and Reynold Nicholson. *The Essential Rumi.*

Schnell, Donald. *The Initiation.*

Slucki, Alex. *The Game of Remembrance.*

Walsh, Neale Donald. *Conversations With God: An Uncommon Dialogue.*

Wright, Machaelle Small. *MAP: The Co-Creative White Brotherhood Medical Assistance Program.*

Yogananda, Paramahansa. *Autobiography of a Yogi.*

ABOUT THE AUTHOR

Ivonne Delaflor, author, teacher, and spiritual practitioner is a certified Parent Talk Trainer and Director of The Parent Talk System in Mexico. As a strong supporter of conscious evolution and God's Realization for all children of the world, Ivonne founded the Mastery Life non-profit organization in 2002, which offers lectures, workshops, and conscious tools for parents to guide children in their full potential as blessed human beings.

Called by her friends a modern female saint for her active work with children at the orphanage La Casita de Cancun, she is a survivor of a near-death experience at the age of 18 that turned her life into a spiritual quest. She began to meet with recognize spiritual teachers worldwide and today shares her passion through offering free workshops and intuitive wisdom for parents in respecting and allowing children to be who they really are.

She is the creator of the twelve-module workshop *Rediscovering Yourself Through Your Personal Power.* She is also the author of *The Soulmate Called God,*

Books I and II, The Positive Child published by iUniverse.com, *La Maestria de La Vida* published in Mexico, and *India, The Journey of a Lifetime*. She is currently working on a workbook entitled *Practical Exercises for the Positive Child*, the profits of which will go to the La Casita de Cancun Orphanage and the book *Mastering Life Book 2; Embracing All as Love*. She is also authoring a book for children that will be donated to the Waldorf School of Santa Barbara, California.

She conducts regular free workshops in Cancun, Mexico and, through her Mastery Life Organization, assists spiritual teachers such as Doreen Virtue, Chick Moorman, Alan Cohen, and many others to share their wisdom in raising the consciousness and awareness that it is through love that children will evolve and teach us their peaceful ways.

Ivonne currently lives with her husband and her two children in California.

0-595-33291-9

www.ingramcontent.com/pod-product-compliance
Lightning Source LLC
Chambersburg PA
CBHW020911290526
45784CB00002BA/507